InstaEnglish

2nd Edition

Student's Book and Workbook

2A

Emma Heyderman
Fiona Mauchline
Patrick Howarth
Patricia Reilly
Olivia Johnston

macmillan education

InstaEnglish
Student's Book and Workbook 2nd Edition
WALKTHROUGH

Check out how your combo edition of the **Student's Book and Workbook** is structured so you can make the most of it!

STUDENT'S BOOK

Your **Student's Book** is made up of a **Starter unit**, **8 regular units**, 4 sets of **review activities**, plus 2 nifty sections: **Digital Literacy** after every 2 units, and **Global Citizenship** after every 4 units.

Starter unit
This two-page unit provides strategic language for you to kick off your studies!

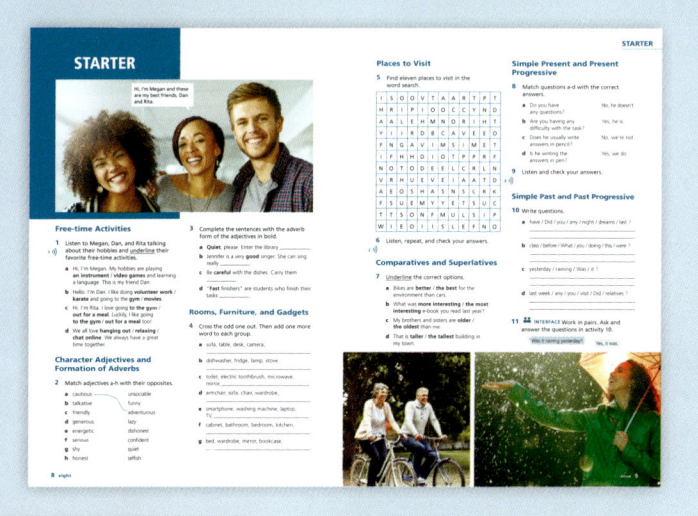

Opener
All regular units open with a visual treat to trigger your first thoughts on the main subject. What's the first thing that pops into your head when you look at it?

VOCABULARY 1
Here you will read, listen to, and look at pictures referring to words or phrases that will help you to explore the unit topic.

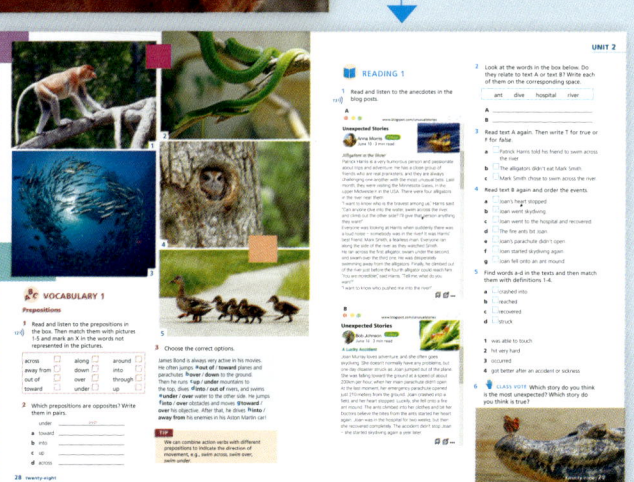

READING 1
Texts of multiple genres provide interesting content to practice your reading skills and introduce relevant language to be explored throughout the unit.

2 two

GRAMMAR 1
Grammar topics that were introduced in the reading text are systematically explored so you can easily work out all the rules and patterns.

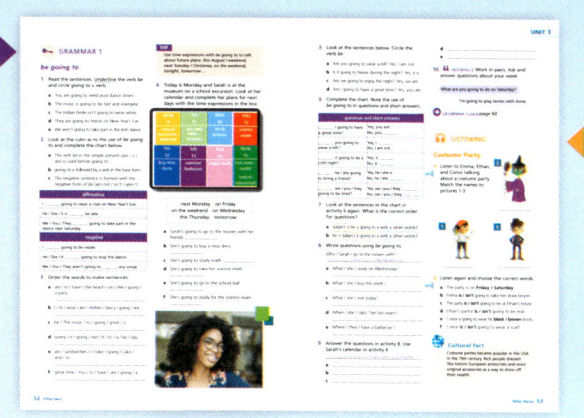

LISTENING
Learn and practice oral comprehension through engaging and contextualized oral texts.

SPEAKING
A clearly guided activity will help you practice your speaking skills using functional language in everyday situations. Throughout the levels, as you improve your ability to communicate orally, you will get increasing contact with real-life oral text genres.

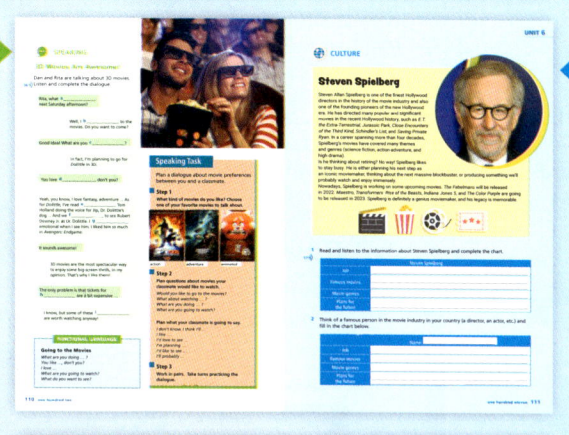

CULTURE
Discover cultural aspects of everyday life in English-speaking countries across the globe!

VOCABULARY 2
The second vocabulary set provides more words and phrases to allow you to go further into the unit topic.

READING 2
The second reading text digs further into the main topic and provides more language to be explored.

GRAMMAR 2
A new grammar topic is introduced in the same contextualized and systematic way seen in **Grammar 1**.

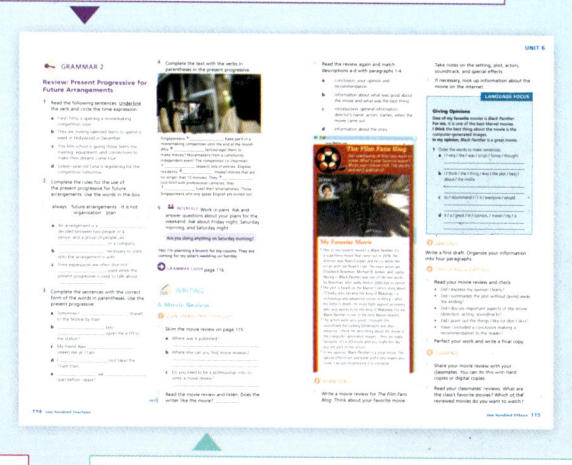

CLIL
In every odd-numbered unit, the **Grammar 2** section is accompanied by the **CLIL** section, for you to integrate your learning of the English language with other school subjects through fun texts and activities.

WRITING
In even-numbered units, the **Grammar 2** section is followed by the **Writing** section, where you are supported every step of the way to practice your writing skills in a range of text genres.

three 3

GRAMMAR GUIDE
This is a reference section for all the grammar topics explored in the unit.

VOCABULARY IN PICTURES
Have fun reviewing all the words and phrases learned in the **Vocabulary** sections, all richly illustrated!

PROGRESS CHECK
Once you complete the unit, cut this page out and close your book. Do the activities and check your overall progress. Then go back to the **Grammar Guide** and the **Vocabulary in Pictures** pages and revise anything you missed.

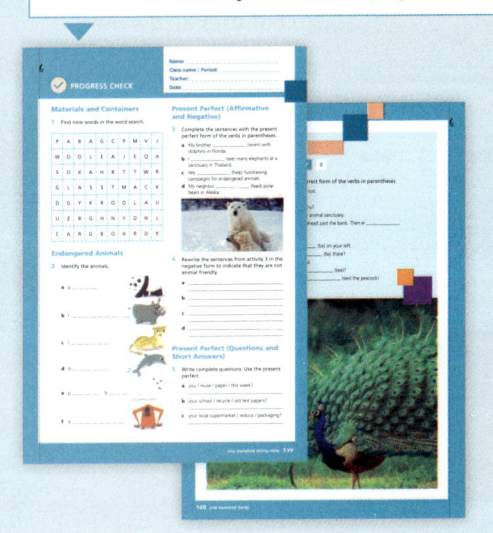

Review
Review the vocabulary and grammar from the previous two units starting with a game!

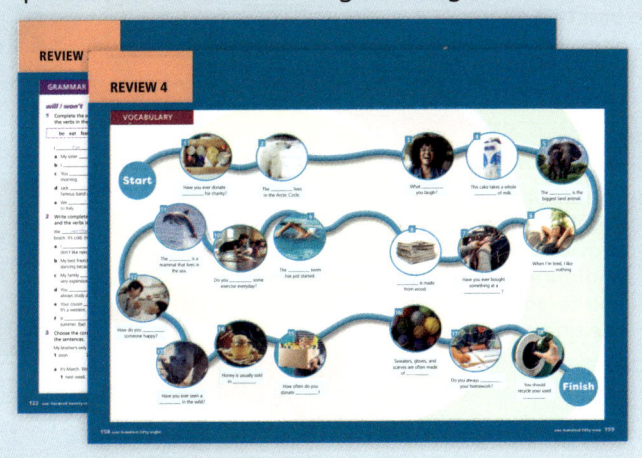

DIGITAL LITERACY
Do you think you use digital technology wisely? Follow siblings Lily and Daniel in a manga-style comic and see how they interact *with* and *through* the digital universe while reflecting about their (and your) relationship with the "digital."

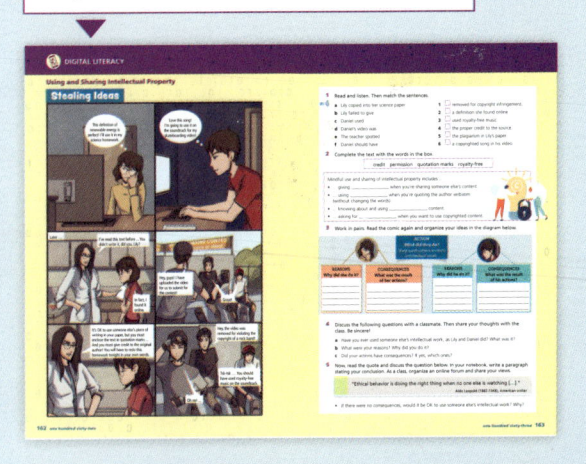

GLOBAL CITIZENSHIP
All of us need to nurture the perception that we are part of the same world. We need to build knowledge and develop skills to live together in the best possible way. That's what this section is all about!

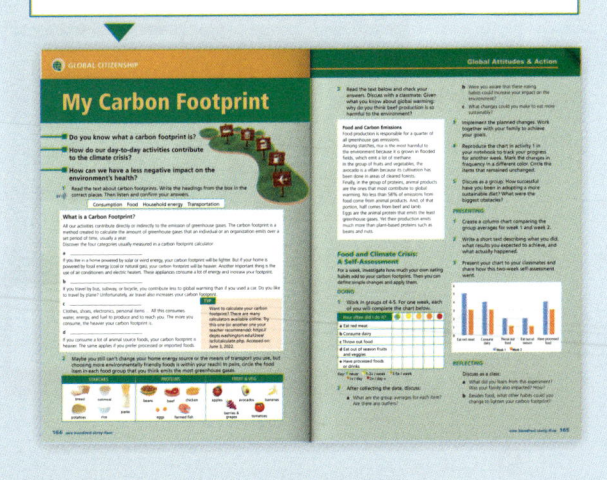

The **TIP, READING STRATEGY, PRONUNCIATION, CULTURAL FACT, FUNCTIONAL LANGUAGE, LANGUAGE FOCUS, CLASS VOTE,** and **INTERFACE** features will make your learning process more practical and effective.

WORKBOOK

The **Workbook** offers target-language practice and additional study material (consolidation and extension). It can be used as homework, independent study, or extra classroom practice. Some of the sections correspond to sections in the **Student's Book**:

VOCABULARY 1

GRAMMAR 1

VOCABULARY 2

GRAMMAR 2

GRAMMAR CHECK
A text with interesting and curious facts helps you check your reading and language skills.

LISTENING

EXTENSION
This engaging section offers an extra challenge on grammar and vocabulary items.

VOCABULARY PLUS
Learn more words related to the unit topic in a fun way! All words are illustrated.

Wordlist

This offers an alphabetical list of the key vocabulary in the **Student's Book** and from the **Vocabulary Plus** sections. It includes phonetic transcriptions and audio recordings.

DIGITAL OFFERINGS

InstaEnglish **2nd Edition** is a fully flexible course, which means you can study using your physical or your digital books and have access to the exact same content and activities. The digital books contain all the audio tracks and videos embedded. The digital offerings include the **On-the-go Practice** feature, for you to keep learning wherever you are!

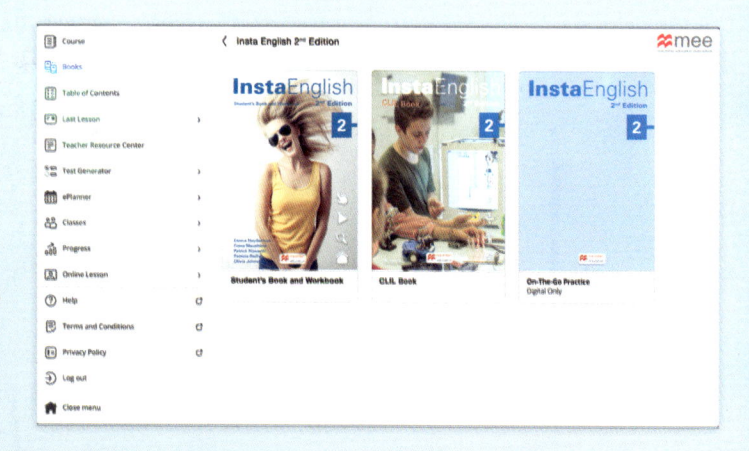

five 5

CONTENTS

UNIT	VOCABULARY	GRAMMAR	READING
Starter 8	Free-time Activities	Character Adjectives and Formation of Adverbs	Rooms, Furniture, and Gadgets
1 TECHNOLOGY 10	1 Contemporary Technologies 12 2 Jobs 18	1 Review: Simple Past 14 2 Review: Past Progressive 20	1 Welcome Back! 13 2 Brain implant helps a blind woman regain her sight 19
2 UNEXPECTED BUT TRUE 26	1 Prepositions 28 2 -ed / -ing Adjectives 34	1 Review: Simple Past and Past Progressive; *when* and *while* 30 2 Present and Past Tenses 36	1 Unexpected Stories 29 2 Mountain Couple Get Home Safely 34
REVIEW 1 42			
3 CELEBRATE! 48	1 Clothes and Accessories 50 2 Weather and Seasons 56	1 *be going to* 52 2 *must / must not* 58	1 Dress Properly for these Celebrations! 51 2 Come to Lollapalooza … But Bring Your Raincoat! 57
4 MAKE A DIFFERENCE 64	1 Jobs 66 2 Health Problems 72	1 *should* (Affirmative and Negative) 68 2 *should* (Questions and Short Answers) 74	1 World Water Day 67 2 Mountain Rescue! 73
REVIEW 2 80			
🌐 GLOBAL CITIZENSHIP – DISCUSSING CONTROVERSIAL TOPICS 86			
IRREGULAR VERBS 166			
WORKBOOK 167			
WORDLIST 234			

LISTENING	SPEAKING	CULTURE	CLIL	WRITING
Places to Visit	Comparatives and Superlatives	Simple Present and Present Progressive		Simple Past and Past Progressive
A Social Network 15	Online Tech 16	Singapore: Planning to Be the Next Tech Hub 17	Science: Microwaves 21	
Shark Attack! 31	An Anecdote 32	Holy Animals of India 33		An Account of an Accident 36

🔤 **DIGITAL LITERACY – DIGITAL NATIVES VERSUS DIGITAL IMMIGRANTS 46**

Costume Party 53	A Birthday Party 54	Birthday Traditions in Jamaica 55	Art: Maori Music 59	
Heroes 69	A Class Presentation 70	Trinidad and Tobago and Its Cultural Relationship with the Ocean 71		An Account for a Local Newspaper 74

🔤 **DIGITAL LITERACY – FACT AND OPINION 84**

STARTER

Hi, I'm Megan and these are my best friends, Dan and Rita.

Free-time Activities

1 Listen to Megan, Dan, and Rita talking about their hobbies and underline their favorite free-time activities.

  a Hi, I'm Megan. My hobbies are playing **an instrument / video games** and learning a language. This is my friend Dan.

  b Hello. I'm Dan. I like doing **volunteer work / karate** and going to the **gym / movies**.

  c Hi. I'm Rita. I love going **to the gym / out for a meal**. Luckily, I like going **to the gym / out for a meal** too!

  d We all love **hanging out / relaxing / chat online**. We always have a great time together.

Character Adjectives and Formation of Adverbs

2 Match adjectives a–h with their opposites.

  a cautious —— unsociable
  b talkative   funny
  c friendly   adventurous
  d generous   lazy
  e energetic   dishonest
  f serious   confident
  g shy   quiet
  h honest   selfish

3 Complete the sentences with the adverb form of the adjectives in bold.

  a **Quiet**, please. Enter the library _____ .

  b Jennifer is a very **good** singer. She can sing really _____ .

  c Be **careful** with the dishes. Carry them _____ .

  d "**Fast** finishers" are students who finish their tasks _____ .

Rooms, Furniture, and Gadgets

4 Cross the odd one out. Then add one more word to each group.

  a sofa, table, desk, camera, _____.

  b dishwasher, fridge, lamp, stove, _____.

  c toilet, electric toothbrush, microwave, mirror, _____.

  d armchair, sofa, chair, wardrobe, _____.

  e smartphone, washing machine, laptop, TV, _____.

  f cabinet, bathroom, bedroom, kitchen, _____.

  g bed, wardrobe, mirror, bookcase, _____.

STARTER

Places to Visit

5 Find eleven places to visit in the word search.

I	S	O	O	V	T	A	A	R	T	P	T
H	R	I	P	I	O	O	C	C	Y	N	D
A	A	L	E	H	M	N	O	R	I	H	T
Y	I	I	R	D	B	C	A	V	E	E	O
F	N	G	A	V	I	M	S	I	M	E	T
I	F	H	H	D	I	O	T	P	P	R	F
N	O	T	O	D	E	E	L	C	R	L	N
V	R	H	U	E	V	E	I	A	A	T	D
A	E	O	S	H	A	S	N	S	C	R	K
F	S	U	E	M	Y	Y	E	T	S	U	C
T	T	S	O	N	F	M	U	L	S	I	P
W	I	E	O	I	I	S	L	E	F	N	O

6 Listen, repeat, and check your answers.

2))

Comparatives and Superlatives

7 <u>Underline</u> the correct options.

a Bikes are **better** / **the best** for the environment than cars.

b What was **more interesting** / **the most interesting** e-book you read last year?

c My brothers and sisters are **older** / **the oldest** than me.

d That is **taller** / **the tallest** building in my town.

Simple Present and Present Progressive

8 Match questions a-d with the correct answers.

a Do you have any questions? — No, he doesn't.

b Are you having any difficulty with the task? — Yes, he is.

c Does he usually write answers in pencil? — No, we're not.

d Is he writing the answers in pen? — Yes, we do.

9 Listen and check your answers.

3))

Simple Past and Past Progressive

10 Write questions.

a have / Did / you / any / night / dreams / last ?
_____
_____

b class / before / What / you / doing / this / were ?
_____
_____

c yesterday / raining / Was / it ?
_____
_____

d last week / any / you / visit / Did / relatives ?
_____
_____

11 **INTERFACE** Work in pairs. Ask and answer the questions in activity 10.

Was it raining yesterday? — Yes, it was.

nine 9

1

TECHNOLOGY

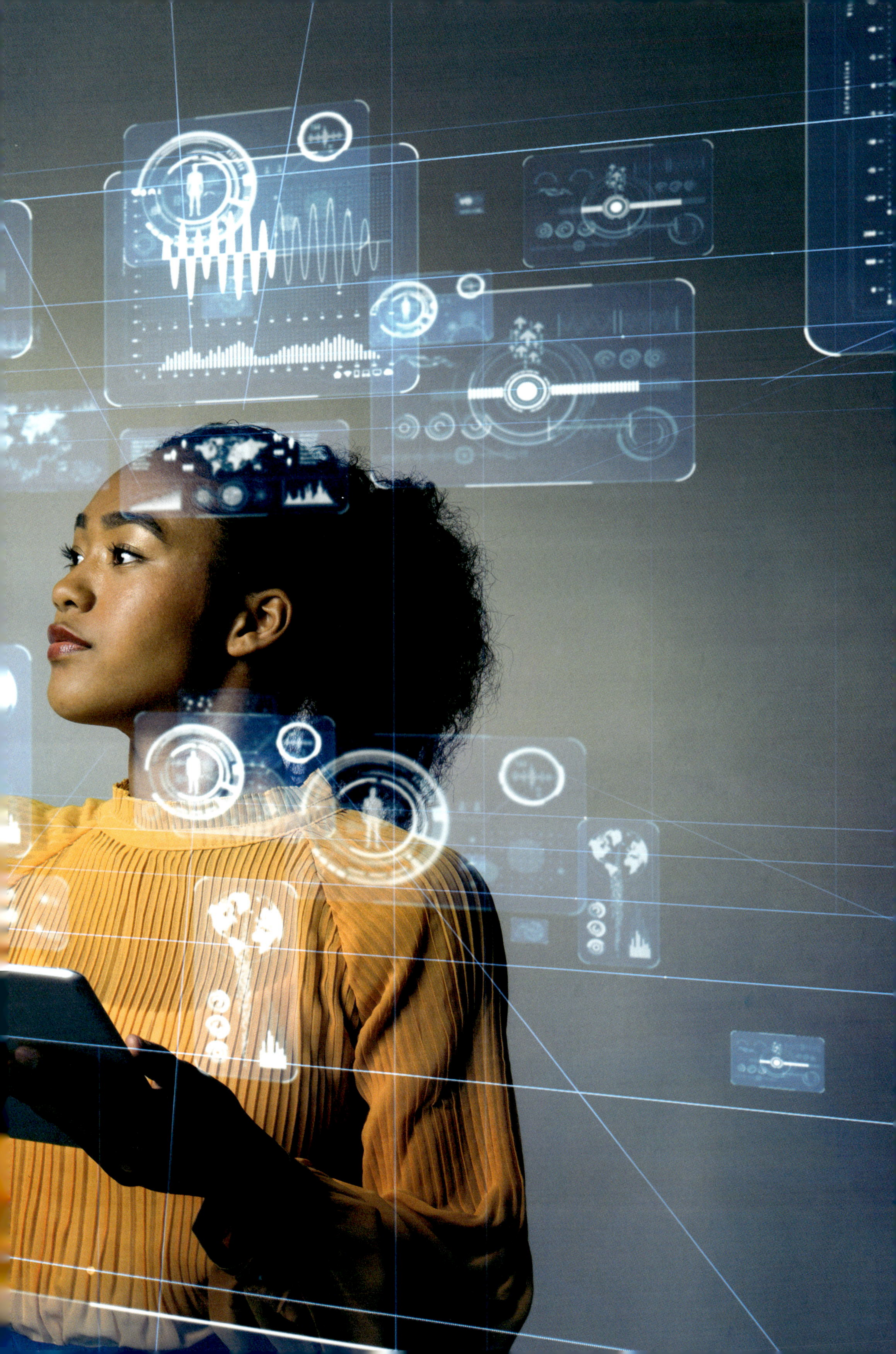

VOCABULARY 1

Contemporary Technologies

1. Match pictures 1-6 with the words in the box. Mark an X next to the words that are not in the pictures.

   > artificial intelligence (AI) ☐
   > augmented reality (AR) ☐
   > cloud storage services ☐   cryptocurrency ☐
   > internet of things (IoT) ☐
   > metaverse ☐   video conferencing ☐
   > virtual reality (VR) ☐

2. Listen and repeat.
   4))

3. Complete the definitions with the correct words from activity 1.

   ___Internet of things___ is the interconnection of computing devices embedded in everyday objects, enabling them to send and receive data.

   a A _____ is a private digital currency (not issued by any government) protected by cryptography.

   b _____ is a computer-generated environment with scenes, people, objects, and sounds that seem real, making the user feel he or she is physically present in a non-physical world.

   c _____ is the simulation of human intelligence in machines that are programmed to perform human activities.

   d _____ is a technology that superimposes text, pictures, or sound on a user's view of the real world.

   e A _____ is an immersive and hyper-realistic virtual environment, where people can interact virtually using 3D avatars and cryptocurrencies.

UNIT 1

READING 1

1 Look at the text below. What is it?

   a The first page of a newsletter.   **b** The cover of a magazine.

NEW HORIZON SCHOOL

Welcome Back!

Dear Students,
During the COVID-19 crisis, you had to adapt to remote learning. We know that only seeing your classmates and teachers on screen was a challenge for you. We're sure you all celebrated the return to in-person learning.
We on the New Horizon School Board also love seeing our students back in the classrooms and hallways. However, we believe that some technologies that became popular during quarantine are here to stay.
Discover the technology advances we prepared for you to enjoy this school year.

- VR laboratory: Our lab now has virtual reality headsets. Your Robotics and Science classes will get more exciting. You will be able to manipulate machines, atoms, genes … and create everything your imagination allows.

- Interactive whiteboards: All of our classrooms are now equipped with interactive whiteboards. Your teachers can use them to access files stored in the cloud at any time. You can interact with lessons and solve problems right on the screen.

- Augmented reality app: On excursions to museums and natural parks, you will use our augmented reality app. Just point your smartphone at a statue, for example, and you'll be able to read the information about it entered by your History teacher.

We wish you the very best for this school year. Make technology your ally in learning!

Larry Schon
Principal

IN THIS ISSUE

pages 2-3
Back to School Essentials

page 4
Safety Reminders

pages 5-6
School Calendar

page 7
Contact Information

page 8
Get Involved

---

2 Read the text and listen to the information. Then choose the correct options.

   a The text was written …
      ☐ during the COVID-19 crisis.
      ☐ after the COVID-19 crisis.

   b New Horizon School students are …
      ☐ starting the school year.
      ☐ returning to in-person learning.

   c The text is signed by …
      ☐ the teachers.
      ☐ the school principal.

   d The author's main objective is to …
      ☐ present the new technologies available to the students.
      ☐ teach students to use the new technologies.

   e The school calendar …
      ☐ needs to be picked up at school.
      ☐ is also in the newsletter.

3 Read the text again. Then write T for *true* or F for *false*.

   a ☐ According to the principal, students prefer remote learning.

   b ☐ The principal speaks for the school's governing board.

   c ☐ During the COVID-19 crisis, students at New Horizon School were taught via videoconferencing.

   d ☐ The VR headset will be used for Robotics and Science learning.

   e ☐ The augmented reality app can only be used inside the school.

READING STRATEGY

In a written text, not all information is explicit. To understand it well, you need to infer some information from what the author says.

4 **CLASS VOTE** Which of the technologies available at New Horizon School do you find most exciting?

GRAMMAR 1

Review: Simple Past

1. Read the sentences below. Circle the irregular verbs and underline the regular verbs.

   a When I passed my exams, my parents gave me an e-book reader.

   b I played a lot of video games when I was younger. They were addictive!

   c I didn't have a cell phone until I was twelve.

   d Did your parents give you anything special on your birthday? Was it nice?

2. Look at the charts below. Then complete the sentences that follow them.

was / were (Simple Past of be)	
+	I / He / She / It **was** great! We / You / They **were** twelve.
–	I / He / She / It **wasn't** popular. We / You / They **weren't** young.
?	**Was** I / he / she / it nice? **Were** we / you / they young?

Simple Past		
	regular verbs	irregular verbs
+	I **passed** my exams.	They **gave** me a smart TV.
–	He **didn't play** computer games.	She **didn't have** a cell phone.
?	**Did** you **save** any money?	**Did** you **get** anything special on your birthday?

   a The past forms of the verb *be* are _____ for I / he / she / it and _____ for we / you / they.

   b *Was / wasn't* and *were / weren't* are used in affirmative, _____, and _____ sentences.

   c *-ed* or *-d* are usually added to the base form of regular verbs in the _____ form.

   d In questions and negative sentences, the auxiliary _____ is used to form the simple past tense.

3. Complete the questions with the simple past tense of the verbs in parentheses.

   a What _____ (be) early cell phones like?

   b What _____ Martin Cooper _____ (invent)?

   c _____ the portable phone _____ (need) to be powered through a car?

   d How long _____ it _____ (take) for it to be available to the public?

   e What _____ Motorola _____ (do)?

   f When _____ Apple _____ its first iPhone? (release)

4. Match the answers below with the questions in activity 3 and find out about the history of cell phones.

   ☐ He invented a portable handheld phone.

   ☐ No, it didn't.

   ☐ It took ten years.

   ☐ In 2007.

   ☐ They were "car phones" – two-way radios used by taxi drivers and emergency services.

   ☐ Motorola introduced the first public cell phone.

5. Complete the text with the simple past form of the verbs in parentheses.

The World Wide Web

Thirty years ago, there **a** _____ (not be) a World Wide Web and there **b** _____ (not be) any social networking sites. By 1994, there **c** _____ (be) about a hundred important websites – today there are billions! The web **d** _____ (develop) when search engines such as Google **e** _____ (become) available and more people **f** _____ (get) high-speed broadband in their homes. Today, it is hard to imagine life without the web.

Cultural fact

Top three countries with highest number of internet users:
1st – China (1 billion)
2nd – India (658 million)
3rd – the USA (307 million)

UNIT 1

6 Ashley made a list of things to do yesterday. Look at the list and write sentences about what she did / didn't do.

+	✕

- ✕ Buy a new e-book.
- ✓ Create a music playlist for my next vacation.
- ✓ Upload some photos to a cloud storage service.
- ✓ Check the comments on my latest post on Instagram.
- ✕ Send two emails.

She didn't buy a new e-book.
_____
_____
_____
_____
_____
_____

7 Read the spelling rules for the simple past of regular verbs. Complete the chart with the simple past form of the verbs in the box.

create	plan	play	plug
sign	store	try	upload

For most verbs, add -ed:	_____ _____
For verbs that end in e, add -d:	_____ _____
For verbs that end in a consonant + y, preceded by a consonant, omit the y and add -ied:	_____ _____
For verbs that end in a vowel + y, just add -ed:	_____ _____
For verbs that end in a stressed vowel + a consonant (except w, x, or y), double the final consonant and add -ed:	_____ _____

8 👥 **INTERFACE** Work in pairs. Ask and answer questions about last weekend. Use the ideas in the box or your own ideas.

create a playlist	join the metaverse
play online games	shop online
use augmented reality	use cryptocurrency
use social network	use streaming services

Did you shop your cell phone online?

Yes, I did. I bought it on Monday and the cell phone arrived on Wednesday. It was really fast!

➡ **GRAMMAR GUIDE** page 22

🎧 LISTENING

A Social Network

1 Read the sentences in activity 2 and check the meaning of any unknown words. Can you guess any of the answers?

2 Tom is doing an oral presentation about a very known social network. Listen to him and choose the correct options.

a ... computer science students started Facebook.
  1 Two   2 Three   3 Four

b Facebook became available to anyone over thirteen years old in ...
  1 2004.   2 2005.   3 2006.

c Facebook is not permitted in ...
  1 schools.
  2 some countries.
  3 all offices.

d Facebook is ... Instagram.
  1 more popular than
  2 not as popular as
  3 as popular as

e The new verb "unfriend" means ...
  1 to argue with a friend online.
  2 to delete a friend from your friend list.
  3 to find friends using your list of friends.

SPEAKING

Online Tech

Rob and his dad Doug are shopping Rob's birthday present online. Listen to them and complete the dialogue.

7 🔊

Gee! Look at these **a** _____, dad! They look cool, don't they?

They really do.

Look, dad, wireless, great noise-cancelling tech, and top-notch battery life!

I see, but they are expensive!!! So different from the ones sold when I was your age, in the 1980s.

What **b** _____ they like, dad?

Well, the 1980s **c** _____ the Walkman era, so we **d** _____ small, portable, and usually cheap headphones.

Walkman??? What was that?

It **e** _____ a small cassette player that **f** _____ in your pocket, but it was cool because people **g** _____ their own music tapes by mixing together songs that they **h** _____ off of different albums.

So old! Nowadays we use digital music services that connect us to millions of songs from all over the world!

Yeah, I know ... Well, let's get back to this new era, then. Which headphones do you want?

FUNCTIONAL LANGUAGE

Talking about Tech Gadgets
Look at this / these ... It's / They're cool!
What was it / were they like ... ?
Nowadays it is / they are ...

Speaking Task

Create a dialogue between you and your parents or guardians about a modern technology.

■ **Step 1**

Decide which technology you are going to talk about. Choose from the ones below or use your own ideas.

Internet of things

Virtual reality headset

Home assistant

Wireless earbuds

■ **Step 2**

Think about how it was without this technology in the past. If necessary, search some information about the concept or gadget on the internet.

■ **Step 3**

Take turns practicing your dialogue.

UNIT 1

🌐 CULTURE

Singapore: Planning to Be the Next Tech Hub

Singapore, a city-state, is a multiracial and multicultural island country with ethnic Indians, Chinese, and Malays who are working hard to become Asia's next economic model. Under the leadership of its founder and "Minister Mentor" Lee Kuan Yew, Singapore continues to be an icon of economic growth and political stability.

Singapore is identifying key sectors where it can join technology with the great market opportunities of Asia: biomedicine, clean technology, and digital media.

As to biomedicine, what Singapore has in mind is to focus on nanomedicine to try to detect cancer in its early stages, to offer computerized medical devices to help the recovery of stroke patients, and to provide sustainable manufacturing of synthesized drugs. Singaporeans have an outstanding health service and the result is the lowest child mortality rate in the world and high life expectancy: almost 84 years, the fifth highest in the world.

Clean technology is also a target: water desalination, electric vehicles, and hybrid buses are part of the project. Artificial intelligence is also receiving investment.

Singapore is totally connected, globally aware, and ready for more. Singaporeans are not afraid of taking strategic risks to reinvent their economy. The growth rate in this tiny city reached 18% – the highest in the world –, making Singapore's dreams come true.

1 **Read and listen. Then correct the sentences below.**
8))

   a Singapore used to be Asia's economic model, but it is not anymore.
   _____
   _____

   b Singapore identified two strategic sectors where it can join technology with market opportunities in Asia.
   _____
   _____

   c In biomedicine, Singaporeans just want to focus on nanomedicine to try to detect cancer in its early stages.
   _____
   _____
   _____
   _____

   d Singaporeans have the highest child mortality rate in the world.
   _____
   _____

   e Water desalination, electric vehicles, and hybrid buses are part of the artificial intelligence project.
   _____
   _____

   f Singaporeans don't like to take risks to reinvent their economy.
   _____
   _____

2 **Can you list positive and negative impacts of technology on society?**
   _____
   _____

3 **Has technology influenced any sector in your country? Which sector(s)? How?**
   _____
   _____

VOCABULARY 2

Jobs

1 Match pictures 1-15 with the jobs in the box. Then listen and repeat.

artist ☐	cleaner ☐	construction worker ☐	doctor ☐	firefighter ☐
inspector ☐	journalist ☐	lawyer ☐	mail carrier ☐	police officer ☐
politician ☐	researcher ☐	scientist ☐	teacher ☐	technician ☐

2 Complete the sentences with jobs in activity 1.

a **Hunter Doherty "Patch" Adams** is a famous American _____. He was portrayed in a well-known 1998 movie due to his activism in treating patients rather than their diseases.

b **Jane Goodall** is a famous British _____. She conducted several studies about the behavior of great apes in their natural environment that contributed to preserving wildlife.

c **Peter Tabichi** is a famous Kenyan _____. He was the first African to win The Global Teacher Prize in 2019 for promoting science and peace and helping to address food insecurity.

d **Andy Warhol** was a famous American _____. He was a leading figure in the Pop Art movement for exploring the relationship between art, advertising, and celebrity culture.

e **Jaqueline Goes de Jesus** is a famous Brazilian _____. She led the first Corona virus sequencing in Brazil at the beginning of the COVID-19 Pandemic in 2020.

f **Nelson Mandela** was a famous South African _____. He became the first democratic South Africa's leader in 1994 and won the Nobel Peace Prize for his fight against racial segregation.

3 Put the jobs in activity 1 into four groups. Add one or two more jobs to each group.

-er	-ist	-ian	-or
lawyer,	journalist	politician	doctor

18 eighteen

UNIT 1

READING 2

1 Read the headline of the news report. Write the jobs from activity 1 on page 18 that you expect to find in the text. Then read, listen, and check your answers.

_____

Brain implant helps a blind woman regain her sight

Bernardeta Gómez was working as a biology teacher at a high school in Valencia, Spain, when an inflammation destroyed the bundles of nerves that connect her eyes to her brain. Bernardeta became blind because of the inflammation and for sixteen years she couldn't see at all. Then scientists from Miguel Hernández University of Elche (UMH) told her about a brain implant that could help her regain her sight. Bernardeta accepted to participate in the experiment, and the doctors placed an array of 100 electrodes in her visual cortex. This is the region of the brain where we process visual information.

Bernardeta also received a pair of glasses equipped with a miniature video camera. A specialized software encoded the visual data collected by the camera and sent it to the brain implant.

After surgery

To begin with, the researchers activated the electrodes one by one. "They were showing me a black stripe on a white background when I screamed – 'There!'," recalls Bernardeta. "I wanted to say that the black stripe was there. I was seeing it!"

As her brain became educated, the scientists increased the number of electrodes they activated at a time. "They made it more complex and I started to see narrow bars, wide bars, squares ... and then I learned to distinguish patterns. I got to perceive a human face and the face of a dog." Bernardeta even played a simple Pac-Man-like computer game piped directly into her brain.

Recognition

Bernardeta had the implant for six months, but then had to take it out so that doctors could continue testing. Thanks to her precise descriptions of visual perceptions and her importance to the research, the former teacher was regarded as a co-author on the study.

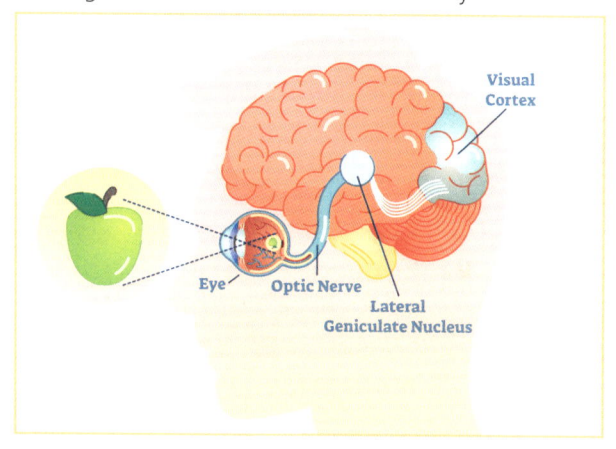

This is how healthy vision works. The prosthesis created by the Spanish scientists restores the connection between the visual cortex and the eye (which is "replaced" by the miniature video camera).

2 Answer the questions.

a What was Bernardeta Gómez's job?
_____
_____

b Why did Bernardeta become blind?
_____
_____
_____

c In which part of Bernardeta's brain did the scientists implant the electrode array?
_____
_____

d What was the first image seen by Bernardeta?
_____
_____

e How was Bernardeta's dedication to the research recognized?
_____
_____
_____

3 Do the activities.

a <u>Underline</u> in the text the words used to refer to the professionals who took care of Bernardeta.

b Check (✓) all that apply: The author of the news report used different words ...
☐ to avoid repeating words.
☐ to retrieve previous ideas.
☐ to talk about different teams.

c Circle in the last paragraph the job Bernardeta used to have.

READING STRATEGY

Texts usually have words that create a link with previously mentioned ideas. For example, the idea of *scientists* is introduced and then other words link to it: *researchers*, *doctors*, etc. Pay attention to these relationships between words.

4 **INTERFACE** Analyze the infographic in the news report. Do you think an artificial eye would solve Bernardeta Gómez's blindness?

GRAMMAR 2

Review: Past Progressive

1 Read the sentences. <u>Underline</u> the verbs in the past progressive form and write A if the sentence is affirmative, N if it is negative, or Q if it is a question.

- **a** ☐ Bernardeta Gómez was working as a biology teacher before she got blind.
- **b** ☐ Bernardeta wasn't using a common pair of glasses.
- **c** ☐ Was Bernardeta seeing after the electrodes implantation?
- **d** ☐ After the implantation, the doctors were showing Bernardeta some images when she realized she was seeing them.
- **e** ☐ Were you reading anything about it?

2 Look at the chart. Then choose the best answer for the questions below.

affirmative	negative	interrogative
I / He / She / It **was working**.	Bernardeta **wasn't using** a common pair of glasses.	**Was** Bernardeta **seeing** after the electrodes implantation?
We / You / They **were reading** about that new experiment.	They **weren't learning** about new technology.	**Were** you **watching** a movie from a streaming service when the lights went off?

- **a** The past progressive is used:
  - ☐ to talk about an action in progress.
  - ☐ to talk about a completed action in the past.
- **b** The past progressive is formed:
  - ☐ with the main verb + -d (or -ed).
  - ☐ with *was* for I / he / she / it and *were* for we / you / they + main verb + -ing form.
- **c** The negative sentence is formed:
  - ☐ by adding *not* to *was* or *were* (*was not* – *wasn't* / *were not* – *weren't*).
  - ☐ by adding *didn't* before the main verb.
- **d** The question is formed:
  - ☐ by adding *did* before the subject.
  - ☐ by placing *was* or *were* before the subject.

3 What was happening when Beth got home? Complete the sentences with the past progressive form of the verbs in parentheses.

When Beth got home …

- **a** her brother Mike _____ (not write) an email, he _____ (watch) TV.
- **b** her parents _____ (look) at a vacation website, they _____ (not prepare) the meal.
- **c** her sister Lisa _____ (not listen) to music on Spotify, she _____ (chat) online.
- **d** her friend Jed _____ (wait) for her, he _____ (not use) the computer.
- **e** the cats Sammy and Fifi _____ (sleep), they _____ (not eating).

4 Complete the text with the past progressive or the simple past form of the verbs in parentheses.

Internet Helps Fight Crime!

Two weeks ago a robber took Dave Reed's laptop when he ____was sleeping____ (sleep). Dave's a writer and he **a** _____ (write) a book at the time – it was all on the computer. Two days later, when Dave **b** _____ (try) to find another computer on the internet, he saw a laptop similar to his old one. Dave went to the seller's house to buy it. When he **c** _____ (look) at the laptop, he realized it was his old one! When the man **d** _____ (not look), Dave sent a message to the police. When the police arrived, Dave **e** _____ (talk) to the man, but he **f** _____ (not buy) the computer. The police found more of Dave's things when they **g** _____ (search) the house. Dave got everything back – thanks to the internet!

5 👥 **INTERFACE** Work in pairs. Ask and answer the question.

> What were you doing at 8pm last night?

> I was watching a movie from a streaming service.

➡ **GRAMMAR GUIDE** page 22

CLIL

SCIENCE

Microwaves

Waves are vibrations that transfer energy from one place to another. Imagine a crowd doing the wave in a sports stadium. The people sit down, until it is their turn to stand up with their arms in the air, and then sit down again.

Like other electromagnetic waves, microwaves travel at the speed of light. Microwave ovens have a magnetron which produces these microwaves at a specific frequency.

The microwaves travel through the food in the oven, and the water molecules in the food start to vibrate. This vibration or movement of the molecules creates heat, which then heats the other molecules in the food.

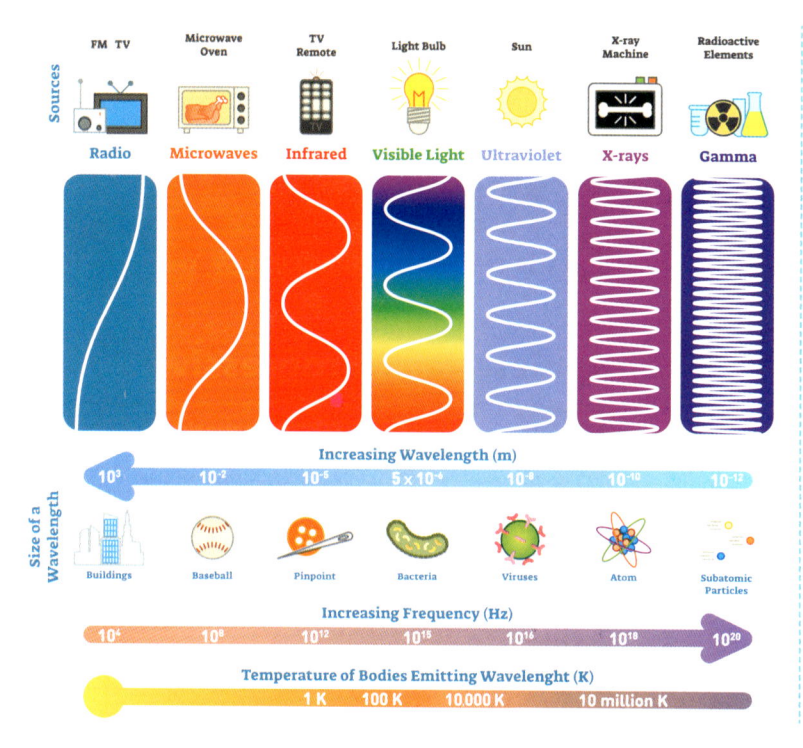

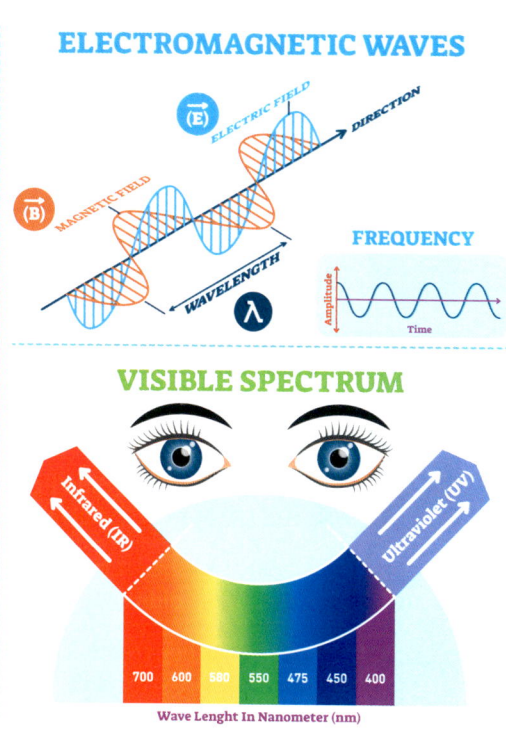

1 Read and listen. Do some online research and answer the question.

Is it possible to cook dry foods like rice or pasta in a microwave oven?

_____

_____

2 Match the instructions to the labels on the diagram.

a ☐ Microwaves make the water molecules vibrate.
b ☐ Microwaves travel through the waveguide to the food.
c ☐ A magnetron generates microwaves.

GRAMMAR GUIDE

Review: Simple Past

- we use the simple past to talk about events in a definite time in the past

was / were (Simple Past of *be*)			
+	I	was	famous.
	You	were	
	He / She / It	was	
	We / You / They	were	
−	I	wasn't	famous.
	You	weren't	
	He / She / It	wasn't	
	We / You / They	weren't	
?	**Was** I / he / she / it famous? Yes, he **was**. No, he **wasn't**.		
	Were we / you / they famous? Yes, we **were**. No, we **weren't**.		

Regular verbs		
+	I / You / He / She / It We / You / They	**created** a playlist.
−	I / You / He / She / It We / You / They	**didn't create** a playlist.
?	**Did** I / you / he / she / it **create** a playlist? Yes, I **did**. / No, I **didn't**.	
	Did we / you / they **create** a playlist? Yes, we **did**. / No, we **didn't**.	

Irregular verbs		
+	I / You / He / She / It We / You / They	**bought** a new e-book.
−	I / You / He / She / It We / You / They	**didn't sent** the email.
?	**Did** I / you / he / she / it **go** to the birthday party? Yes, I **did**. / No, I **didn't**.	
	Did we / you / they **drink** soft drink at the party? Yes, we **did**. / No, we **didn't**.	

Spelling: Simple Past Regular Verbs

- for most verbs, add *-ed*
  invent → invent**ed**
- for verbs that end in *e*, add *-d*
  arrive → arriv**ed**
- for verbs that end in a consonant + *y*, preceded by a consonant, omit the *y* and add *-ied*
  study → stud**ied**
- for verbs that end in a vowel + *y*, just add *-ed*
  play → play**ed**
- for verbs that end in a stressed vowel + a consonant (except *w*, *x*, or *y*), double the final consonant and ad *-ed*
  plug → plug**ged**   refer → refer**red**

Spelling: Simple Past Irregular Verbs

➡ **FOR THE IRREGULAR VERBS LIST**, see page 166

Review: Past Progressive

+	I	was working.
	You	were working.
	He / She / It	was working.
	We / You / They	were working.
−	I	wasn't working.
	You	weren't working.
	He / She / It	wasn't working.
	We / You / They	weren't working.
?	**Was** I / he / she / it **working**? Yes, he **was**. No, he **wasn't**.	
	Were we / you / they **working**? Yes, we **were**. No, we **weren't**.	

- we use the past progressive to describe actions that were in progress in the past

PROGRESS CHECK

Name: _____
Class name / Period: _____
Teacher: _____
Date: _____

Contemporary Technologies

1 Complete the phrases with vowels.

a P L __ Y __ N L __ N __ G __ M __ S

b C R __ __ T __ __ P L __ Y L __ S T

c J __ __ N T H __ M __ T __ V __ R S __

d U S __ V __ R T __ __ L R __ __ L __ T Y

Jobs

2 Complete the sentences with the correct jobs.

a Kathy is a _____. She's investigating new medicine at the moment.

b Joe works in construction. He's a _____.

c Sarah is a _____, she works in a laboratory.

d Frida Kahlo is a famous _____. I like her paintings.

e Jane is a _____. She cleans the school canteen.

f Robert is an _____. He works at the shoe factory.

Review: Simple Past

3 Complete the sentences with the correct form of *be*.

a At 11pm last night Mark _____ in bed.

b Where _____ you at 7pm yesterday?

c They _____ at school yesterday because it _____ Sunday.

d I _____ at home last night because I _____ at my grandma's house. It _____ her birthday.

e _____ Kevin at the party last Saturday?

f No, he _____.

4 Look at Rita's list of things to do yesterday. Then write questions.

✗ Set fridge for vacation.
✓ Schedule video conferencing.
✗ Buy virtual reality headset.
✗ Create login at cloud storage service.
✓ Shop cat food online.

Did Rita set the fridge for her vacation?

a _____
b _____
c _____
d _____

5 Look at Rita's list in activity 4 again and write answers to the questions.

No, she didn't.

a _____
b _____
c _____
d _____

Review: Past Progressive

6 Write questions using the past progressive form. Then answer the questions so they are true for you.

a what / you / do / at 10pm last night?
_____
_____
_____

b what / your parents / do / at 3pm on Sunday?
_____
_____
_____

c you and your friend / watch a movie / at 9pm yesterday?
_____
_____
_____

Grammar Buildup 1

| **1** | 2 | 3 | 4 | 5 | 6 | 7 | 8 |

7 Underline the correct options.

Cell phones are a relatively new invention. Before them, there **a was / were** two-way radios in taxis, police cars, and ambulances, but users **b can't / couldn't** connect to the phone network. In 1910, Lars Ericsson **c installed / was installing** a phone in his car. He **d stopped / was stopping** at different places while he **e traveled / was traveling** across the country. Then he **f connected / was connecting** his phone to the national telephone network with long wires. The first real "mobile" phone system **g started / was starting** in 1956 in Sweden. Today, people **h use / are using** cell phones every day.

UNIT 1

VOCABULARY IN PICTURES

Contemporary Technologies

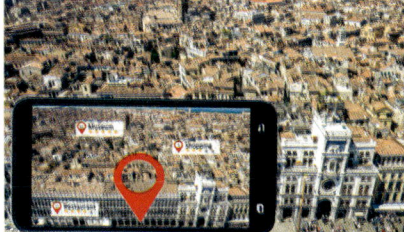

artificial intelligence

augmented reality

cloud storage services

cryptocurrency

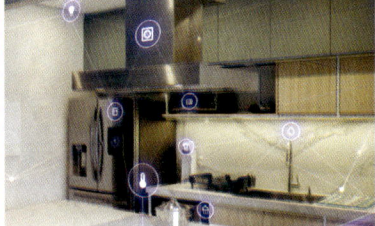

internet of things

metaverse

video conferencing

virtual reality

Jobs

Andy Warhol — artist

cleaner

construction worker

Hunter Doherty "Patch" Adams — doctor

firefighter

inspector

journalist

lawyer

mail carrier

police officer

Nelson Mandela — politician

Jaqueline Goes de Jesus — researcher

Jane Goodall — scientist

Peter Tabichi — teacher

technician

twenty-five 25

2

UNEXPECTED BUT TRUE

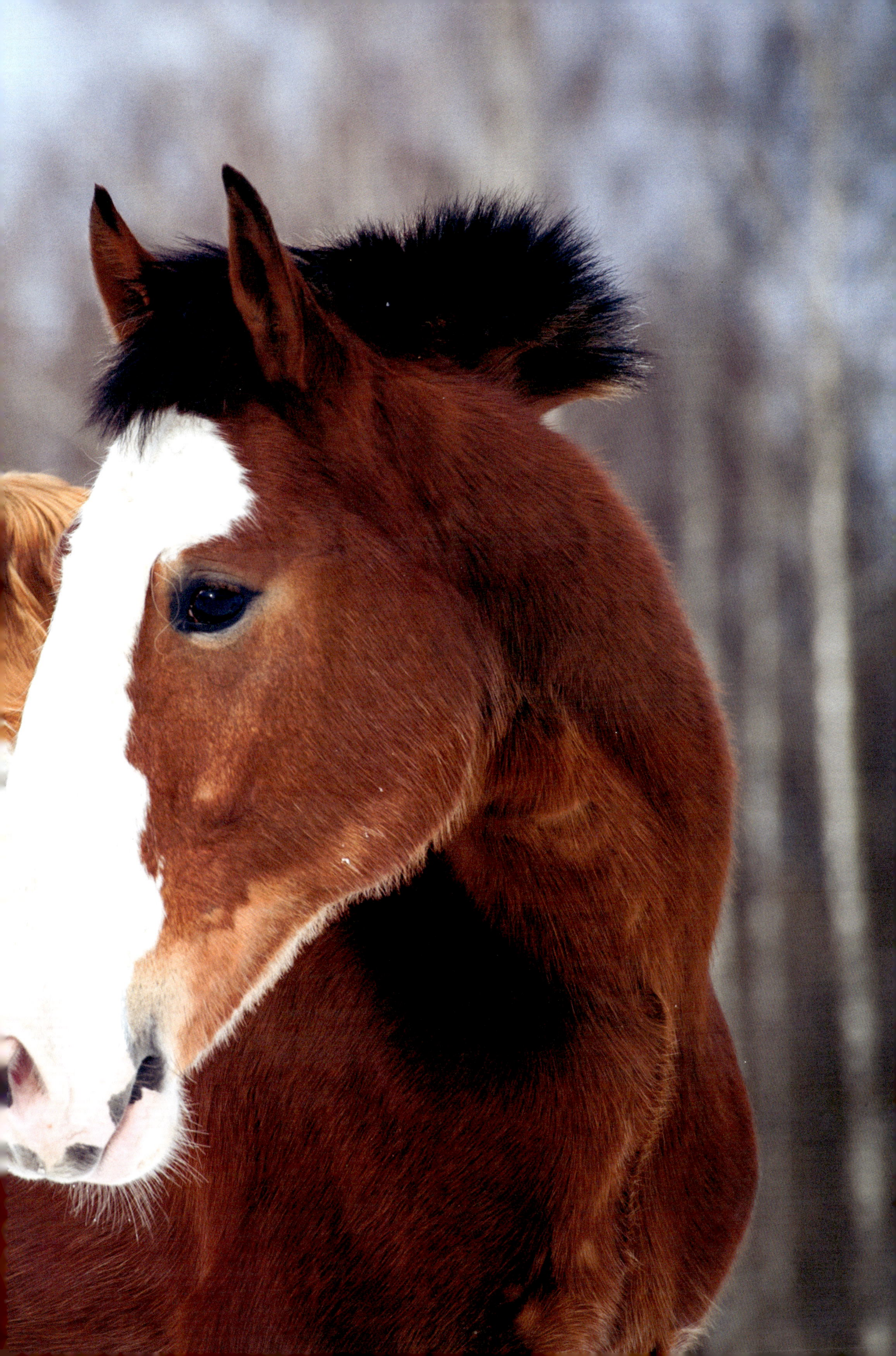

VOCABULARY 1

Prepositions

1 Read and listen to the prepositions in the box. Then match them with pictures 1–5 and mark an X in the words not represented in the pictures.

across ☐	along ☐	around ☐
away from ☐	down ☐	into ☐
out of ☐	over ☐	through ☐
toward ☐	under ☐	up ☐

2 Which prepositions are opposites? Write them in pairs.

under _____over_____
a toward _____
b into _____
c up _____
d across _____

3 Choose the correct options.

James Bond is always very active in his movies. He often jumps **a out of / toward** planes and parachutes **b over / down** to the ground. Then he runs **c up / under** mountains to the top, dives **d into / out of** rivers, and swims **e under / over** water to the other side. He jumps **f into / over** obstacles and moves **g toward / over** his objective. After that, he drives **h into / away from** his enemies in his Aston Martin car!

TIP

We can combine action verbs with different prepositions to indicate the direction of movement, e.g., *swim across, swim over, swim under*.

28 **twenty-eight**

UNIT 2

📘 READING 1

1 Read and listen to the anecdotes in the blog posts.

🔊 13

A

www.blogspot.com/unusualstories

Unexpected Stories

Anna Morris (Follow)
June 10 · 3 min read

Alligators in the River
Patrick Harris is a very humorous person and passionate about trips and adventure. He has a close group of friends who are real pranksters, and they are always challenging one another with the most unusual bets. Last month, they were visiting the Minnesota Gates, in the upper Midwestern in the USA. There were four alligators in the river near them.
"I want to know who is the bravest among us," Harris said. "Can anyone dive into the water, swim across the river, and climb out the other side? I'll give that person anything they want!"
Everyone was looking at Harris when suddenly there was a loud noise – somebody was in the river! It was Harris' best friend, Mark Smith, a fearless man. Everyone ran along the side of the river as they watched Smith. He ran across the first alligator, swam under the second, and swam over the third one. He was desperately swimming away from the alligators. Finally, he climbed out of the river just before the fourth alligator could reach him.
"You are incredible!," said Harris. "Tell me, what do you want?"
"I want to know who pushed me into the river!"

B

www.blogspot.com/unusualstories

Unexpected Stories

Bob Johnson (Follow)
June 16 · 3 min read

A Lucky Accident
Joan Murray loves adventure, and she often goes skydiving. She doesn't normally have any problems, but one day disaster struck as Joan jumped out of the plane. She was falling toward the ground at a speed of about 200km per hour, when her main parachute didn't open. At the last moment, her emergency parachute opened just 210 meters from the ground. Joan crashed into a field, and her heart stopped. Luckily, she fell onto a fire ant mound. The ants climbed into her clothes and bit her. Doctors believe the bites from the ants started her heart again. Joan was in the hospital for two weeks, but then she recovered completely. The accident didn't stop Joan – she started skydiving again a year later.

2 Look at the words in the box below. Do they relate to text A or text B? Write each of them on the corresponding space.

| ant | dive | hospital | river |

A _____
B _____

3 Read text A again. Then write T for *true* or F for *false*.

a ☐ Patrick Harris told his friend to swim across the river.
b ☐ The alligators didn't eat Mark Smith.
c ☐ Mark Smith chose to swim across the river.

4 Read text B again and order the events.

a ☐ Joan's heart stopped.
b [1] Joan went skydiving.
c ☐ Joan went to the hospital and recovered.
d ☐ The fire ants bit Joan.
e ☐ Joan's parachute didn't open.
f ☐ Joan started skydiving again.
g ☐ Joan fell onto an ant mound.

5 Find words a-d in the texts and then match them with definitions 1-4.

a ☐ crashed into
b ☐ reached
c ☐ recovered
d ☐ struck

1 was able to touch
2 hit very hard
3 occurred
4 got better after an accident or sickness

6 ✋ **CLASS VOTE** Which story do you think is the most unexpected? Which story do you think is true?

twenty-nine **29**

GRAMMAR 1

Review: Simple Past and Past Progressive

1 Read the sentences below and write A or B according to the timelines presented.

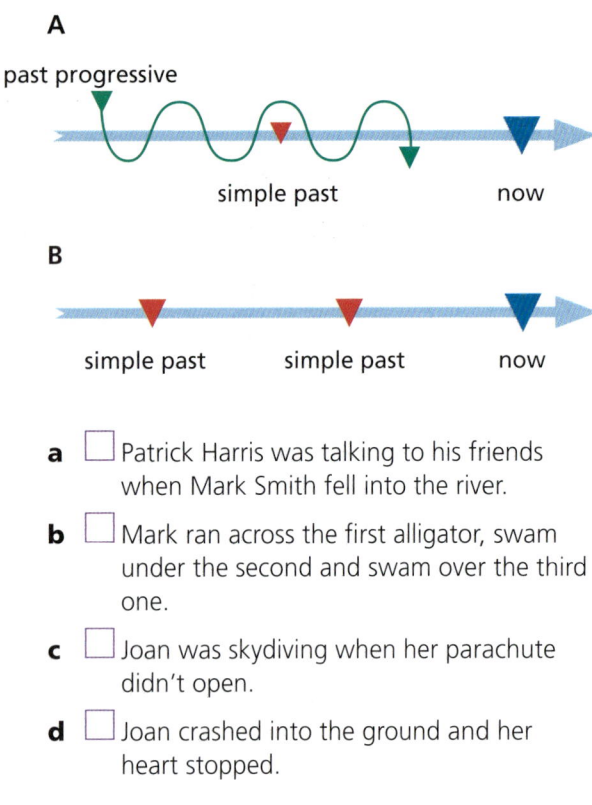

A

past progressive
simple past — now

B

simple past — simple past — now

a ☐ Patrick Harris was talking to his friends when Mark Smith fell into the river.

b ☐ Mark ran across the first alligator, swam under the second and swam over the third one.

c ☐ Joan was skydiving when her parachute didn't open.

d ☐ Joan crashed into the ground and her heart stopped.

2 Look at the examples in the chart below. Then write *simple past* or *past progressive* to complete the following rules as to the use of these verb tenses.

past progressive	simple past
Last month Patrick **was visiting** Minnesota with his friends.	
	The ants **climbed into** Joan's clothes and **bit** her.
Everyone **was looking** at Harris …	… when Mark **fell** into the river.
While Mark **was trying** to cross the river, …	… an alligator **tried** to reach him.

a The most common use of the _____ tense is to talk about something that was happening around a particular time in the past.

b The simple past and the past progressive can be used together. In these cases, the _____ describes a longer action or situation, and the _____ describes the action or events that "interrupt" the situation described in the _____.

3 Choose the correct options.

Last summer, 11-year-old Brennan Hawkins **a went / was going** to Scout Camp. One day, he **b got / was getting** lost in the woods during an activity. Brennan **c survived / was surviving** for four days alone in the woods! When rescuers finally **d found / were finding** Brennan, he **e hid / was hiding** in the trees because he **f didn't recognize / wasn't recognizing** them!

PRONUNCIATION

Sentence Stress

14)) Listen to the sentences and repeat. Which syllables are stressed?

a He was watching a movie.
b They were listening to music.
c He wasn't hiding in the woods.
d Was he talking to David?

when and *while*

4 Note the use of *when* and *while* in the sentences below. Choose the correct information.

when / while
He was running away **when** the bear attacked him.
When the bear saw him, he was taking pictures of the monkeys in the trees.
The bear roared **while** he was running away.
While he was running away, the bear attacked him.

a *While* is usually used before the **past progressive / simple past**.

b *When* is usually used before the **past progressive / simple past**.

c ☐ Use … ☐ Don't use … a comma after a time clause that starts a sentence.

30 thirty

UNIT 2

5 Complete the sentences with the correct form of the verbs in parentheses. Then rewrite the sentences changing *when* and *while*.

He ___was walking___ (walk) in the forest when the dog ___appeared___ (appear).
While he was walking in the forest, the dog appeared.

a While the children _____ (play), they _____ (see) a snake.
_____
_____

b While they _____ (sail) along the coast, there _____ (be) a storm.
_____
_____

c The plane _____ (fly) over the area when the pilot _____ (see) the explorers.
_____
_____

d When I _____ (arrive), the rescuers _____ (look) for the lost girl.
_____
_____

e I _____ (have) an accident while I _____ (drive) home.
_____
_____

f I _____ (see) Hannah when I _____ (be) at the shopping center.
_____
_____

6 Note the use of *when* and *while* in the sentences below. What do they mean? Match sentences a–c with the information below.

a **When** Mark **arrived**, Jane **was cooking** dinner.
b **When** Mark **arrived**, Jane **cooked** dinner.
c **While** Jane **was cooking** dinner, Mark **was taking** a shower.

☐ Jane's and Mark's actions were happening at the same time.
☐ Jane started cooking dinner before Mark arrived.
☐ Jane started cooking dinner after Mark arrived.

➡ **GRAMMAR GUIDE** page 38

LISTENING

Shark Attack!

1 Before listening to a news report, look at the picture and read the words in the box below. What do you think the news report is about?

| attack   beach   bite   bodyboard   hand |
| head   hit   leg   swim   wetsuit |

_____

2 Now listen and check your answer.

3 Listen again. Then write T for *true* and F for *false*. Correct the false sentences.

a ☐ Lydia was swimming when the shark attacked.
_____

b ☐ The shark wasn't very big – it was only about one meter long.
_____

c ☐ The shark was very aggressive.
_____

d ☐ Lydia's brother hit the shark on the head with his bodyboard.
_____

e ☐ The shark let Lydia go and she and her brother ran out of the water.
_____

f ☐ Lydia is planning to swim again at the beach soon.
_____

4 **INTERFACE** Work in pairs. Playing the roles of the reporter and Lydia, ask and answer questions about the shark attack.

> Why did you go to the beach?
>
> I wanted to go bodyboarding.

Cultural fact

Around 21 different species of shark live off the UK coast. Basking sharks are the most common yet they are considered an endangered species and need monitoring, management, and further research to ensure their survival.

💬 SPEAKING

An Anecdote

1 Josh (Speaker 1) is talking to Mark (Speaker 2) about an event at a zoo near Chicago. Read, listen, and answer.
🔊 16

  a What animal was involved in the event?
  _____
  _____

  b Why was the event memorable?
  _____
  _____
  _____
  _____

S1: Mark, did I tell you what I saw at the zoo last Saturday?
S2: No. What happened?
S1: Binti, the gorilla, became a hero! She saved a little boy who fell into Binti's enclosure.
S2: I don't believe it! You know, when animals feel they are in danger, they attack!
S1: You bet! But, in this case, Binti picked the boy up gently and carried him to the door where paramedics were waiting. I couldn't believe my eyes!
S2: Really? How come?
S1: Well, when the boy fell he was unconscious. The keeper said she was training Binti to carry a doll and bring it to her, so Binti developed maternal instincts and probably thought the boy was the doll!
S2: Lucky boy!
S1: Yeah, but Binti's keeper insisted that Binti didn't "rescue" the boy; she was in no immediate danger and the other gorillas weren't around.
S2: Fortunately, things turned out all right!

> **TIP**
> An anecdote is a short, interesting or amusing story about a real incident or a person.

2 **Reported speech** is when we tell someone what another person said. For example, Mark tells Josh: "The keeper said she was training Binti to carry a doll."

  a Underline other example of reported speech in the dialogue.

  b What verb was used to introduce the other person's speech?
  _____

  c Why is it common to use reported speech when we are telling an anecdote?
  _____

> **FUNCTIONAL LANGUAGE**
> **Telling an Anecdote**
> *Did I tell you … ?*
> *What happened?*
> *Really? How come?*

Speaking Task

Tell an anedocte to a friend.

■ **Step 1**
Think of a remarkable incident that you have experienced and plan to tell a classmate about it.

■ **Step 2**
Think about the specific details of the anecdote and how to tell it.
Did I tell you about … ?
It was so frightening / interesting …
I was so embarrassed / bored …

Think about your classmate's questions and reactions.
Really? How come?
What happened?
Where were you?
You were lucky / stupid / brave …

If you want to use reported speech, think of different verbs to introduce what other people said.
He / she said / insisted / exclaimed / asked / shouted …

Take notes and rehearse a few times. Try to tell the story with emotion.

■ **Step 3**
Work with a classmate. Tell your anecdotes to each other.

When it's your turn to listen, pay attention to your classmate's words and make comments that are consistent with the story being told.

CULTURE

Holy Animals of India

It may sound strange to Western civilization, but in India animals are considered sacred. This secular country strongly believes in the divinity of animals, especially those referred to in Indian mythology and ancient Indian culture.

The Cow
The cow is the holiest animal in India. It is treated as a god who has taken the form of an animal, a gift of the gods to the people. For that reason, slaughtering is banned all over the country. However, studies have shown that ancient Indians ate beef in ancient times. It was a myth, composed between 300 BC and AD 300, that led to the transition to not eating cows.

The Elephant
The elephant in India is part of Hindu culture. It is the god (divinity) of success and education. In the past it was used as an instrument of war. Nowadays, during festival seasons it is decorated and worshiped.

The Monkey
The monkey is considered to be a form of Hanuman – the god of power and strength. The biggest monkey, called langur or Hanuman langur, is the most sacred in India.

The Snake
Several old cultures worship serpents. The Indian cobra is the most sacred snake in India and is revered by Hindus. Snake charmers are followers of Lord Shiva, the Hindu god who wears a king cobra around his neck.

The Royal Bengal Tiger
The Royal Bengal tiger, in all its strength and glory, is not only a sacred animal but also the national symbol of India. Indians also worship the tiger because they are afraid of it.

---

1 Read and listen to the information. Then write the names of the corresponding animals in the spaces below.

<u>The Royal Bengal Tiger</u>: It is the national symbol of India.

a _____: Its meat cannot be eaten.
b _____: It is revered by Hindus, and the Hindu god, Lord Shiva, wears one around his neck.
c _____: It is the god of success and education.
d _____: It is the god of power and strength.
e _____: It was used as an instrument of war.
f _____: Indian people ate its meat in ancient times.

2 Different animals mean different things in countries all over the world. Are any animals worshiped in your country?
_____
_____

3 How are animals (wild / farm / pets) treated in your country?
_____
_____

ABC VOCABULARY 2

-ed / -ing Adjectives

1 Look at the pictures and choose the correct word.

  a The **couple** / **mountains** are frighten**ed**.

  b The **couple** / **mountains** are frighten**ing**.

2 Complete the rules with *-ed* or *-ing*.

  a We use _____ adjectives to describe how we feel.

  b We use _____ adjectives to describe the thing or person that causes the feeling.

3 Complete the chart with the verbs in the box below.

~~annoy~~ bore excite frighten
interest surprise tire worry

verb	-ing form	-ed form
annoy	annoying	annoyed

4 Choose the correct words.

  a John is **bored** / **boring** because the movie is **bored** / **boring**.

  b The results of the experiments are very **surprised** / **surprising**. The scientists are **worried** / **worrying**.

  c I'm **annoyed** / **annoying** because my friend is late – again! It's very **annoyed** / **annoying** when people are always late.

  d We're **tired** / **tiring** because it's very late, but the documentary is really **interested** / **interesting**.

  e They are **frightened** / **frightening** of spiders. They think spiders are **frightened** / **frightening**.

5 Listen, check, and repeat.

18))

📖 READING 2

1 Look at the pictures above and answer the questions.

  a How do you think the people felt in the situation?
  _____
  _____

  b What do you think happened to the people?
  _____
  _____

2 Match items a-e with their synonyms.

  a get stuck   ☐ care for
  b look after   ☐ come back
  c return   ☐ become trapped
  d work   ☐ be able to do something
  e manage   ☐ function

UNIT 2

3 Read and listen to the news report. Then answer the questions.

a What happened to Keith and Jennifer on the way home?
_____

b Why didn't they use their phones?
_____

c Who did they think about while they were trying to move the car?
_____

d Who did they call on the way home?
_____

e Are they planning to go again next year?
_____

Mountain Couple Get Home Safely

Keith and Jennifer Lee live in Oregon, in the USA. Every year they go to the mountains. They don't usually have any problems, but last year things were different. They drove up to the mountains as usual, but as they were driving home they suddenly got stuck in the snow.

Unfortunately, their phones weren't working so high up. It was a worrying situation. While they were trying to move the car, they thought about their four children, aged 8 to 18. A friend, Sophie Smith, was taking care of the children. When the Lees didn't return, Sophie became worried. She called the police and a search began.

Two days later Keith finally managed to move the car. They were driving home when they heard about the search for them on the radio. They were surprised. They called the police and then called Sophie. "They're safe. They're coming home!," Sophie shouted when she heard the news. Everyone was delighted.

Keith is planning to go back to the mountains again next year, but Jennifer doesn't want to go. It was a frightening experience for her – she thinks they should stay in town.

4 Find synonyms for these adjectives in the text.

    distressing   _worrying_

a pleased   _____
b shocked   _____
c anxious   _____
d terrifying   _____

5 Keith and Jennifer spent two days stuck in the snow. What do you think they did during that time?
_____
_____
_____
_____
_____

GRAMMAR 2

Present and Past Tenses

1 Look at the chart and match the sentences to the information below.

present and past tenses
a Every year Keith and Jennifer **go** to the mountains.
b They**'re coming** home!
c They **were driving** home when they got stuck.
d Keith finally **managed** to move the car.

☐ It describes a habit.

☐ It refers to an action in progress in the past.

☐ It describes something happening now.

☐ It describes a completed action in the past.

2 Refer to the chart in activity 1 and use the verb tenses in the box to complete the information below.

past progressive	present progressive
simple past	simple present

a It describes a habit: _____.

b It refers to an action in progress in the past: _____.

c It describes something happening now: _____.

d It describes a completed action in the past: _____.

3 Read the text *Mountain Couple Get Home Safely* again and write suitable questions for these answers.

a Where _____?
Keith and Jennifer Lee live in Oregon, in the USA.

b What _____
_____?
They were driving home when they got stuck in the snow.

c _____?
No, their phones weren't working.

d Who _____?
Sophie called, and the search began.

e _____
_____?
No, only Keith is planning to go back to the mountains next year.

4 Complete the text with the correct form of the verbs in parentheses.

Vanessa Horrocks ___was watching___ (watch) TV in her apartment when she
a _____ (hear) a strange noise in the bathroom. She **b** _____ (go) to check. She **c** _____ (have) a terrible shock when she **d** _____ (see) a two-meter-long python in the toilet. "The snake **e** _____ (try) to get out of the toilet," she **f** _____ (tell) our reporter, "so I **g** _____ (run) out of the bathroom because I certainly **h** _____ (not want) to try and catch it. Then I **i** _____ (call) Fred, our building manager. He **j** _____ (arrive) pretty quickly. He **k** _____ (catch) the snake and **l** _____ (take) it away." Vanessa still **m** _____ (feel) nervous when she uses her bathroom. "And I always **n** _____ (put) the toilet lid down now," she said.
Building manager Fred Murray told us: "Pet pythons sometimes **o** _____ (escape) and **p** _____ (live) in the water systems of large apartment blocks. We **q** _____ (look for) the python's owner now. At the moment it **r** _____ (live) in a cage in my apartment, but it **s** _____ (grow) very fast."

➡ **GRAMMAR GUIDE** page 38

✏️ WRITING

An Account of an Accident

① EXPLORING THE CONTEXT

1 Skim the text on page 37 and underline the correct options.

a This account was published **on a blog / on a news website**.

b *To witness* mean **to escape with life from something / to see something happen**.

2 Read and listen. Then put the pictures on page 37 in the correct order.

20 🔊

UNIT 2

www.myeverydayadventuresblog.com

My Everyday Adventures

I witnessed an accident!
April, 12 • by Sam Lee

Hi, guys! Last Saturday evening I witnessed an accident, can you believe it? Let me tell you how it happened ...
I was walking into town with my friend Jenny. It was raining really hard because there was a terrible storm. It was a bit frightening, and we were thinking about going back home.
Suddenly, there was a loud noise and a big tree branch fell down into the road! We were trying to move the branch when a car appeared. The driver wasn't driving very fast, but he didn't see the branch and he drove into it. I ran to the car and looked inside. The driver wasn't conscious and there was blood on his head. Meanwhile, Jenny called an ambulance.
An ambulance arrived quite quickly and took the man to the hospital. Then, a reporter arrived when we were leaving, so we told her about the accident. The next day our story was in the newspaper – it was really exciting!

3 Read the text again. Then answer.

  a What adjectives does Sam use to describe the situation?
  _____

  b Besides the accident itself, what else made the event remarkable?
  _____
  _____

4 Match each paragraph to its purpose.

  a 1st paragraph
  b 2nd paragraph
  c 3rd paragraph
  d 4th paragraph

  ☐ Tell the accident itself.
  ☐ Introduce the account.
  ☐ Tell what happened after the accident.
  ☐ Describe the setting and the people involved.

2 PLANNING

1 Imagine that you have a blog. You will write and share an account of an accident.

2 Think of an imaginary or a real accident. When, where, and how did it happen? Make notes.

LANGUAGE FOCUS

Time Expressions

Read these sentences.
- We were talking. **Suddenly**, the phone rang.
- The police evacuated the area. **Meanwhile**, the firefighters tried to stop the fire.
- We called an ambulance. **Then**, we helped the accident victims.

1 Find in the text examples of the words in bold.
2 Write *suddenly*, *meanwhile*, or *then*.
  a The rescuers climbed down to the boy. _____, they took him to the helicopter.
  b We were walking through the jungle. _____, we saw a tiger!
  c I started making a fire. _____, my friends looked for more wood.

3 WRITING

1 Write your first draft. Use your notes from Step 2 and Sam's account to help you.
2 Organize the story into four paragraphs.
3 Use adjectives to describe the events.
4 Use time expressions.

4 CHECKING & EDITING

1 Exchange your account with a classmate's:
   - Can you identify the sequence of events?
   - Can you recognize the emotions that the accident provoked?
2 Consider your classmate's opinions and make a final copy of your work.

5 SHARING

1 Join three classmates. None of them should have worked with you in Step 4.
2 Listen to each other's accounts and guess which are true and which are imaginary.

GRAMMAR GUIDE

Review: Simple Past and Past Progressive

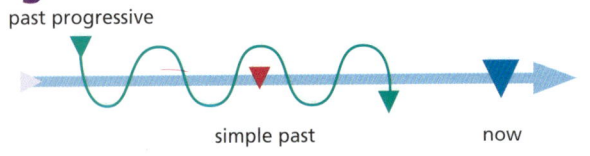

She **was falling** toward the ground when her main parachute **didn't open**.

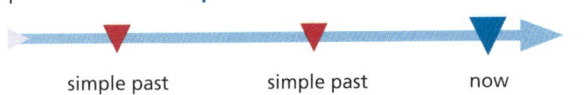

Joan **crashed** into the ground and her heart **stopped**.

- we often use the past progressive and the simple past in the same sentence
  When she **was falling**, her parachute **didn't open**.
- we use the past progressive for actions in progress in the past and the simple past for events which interrupt the action in progress
  John **was watching** TV when Beth **arrived**.
- we also use the simple past for a sequence of actions in the past
  Joan **crashed** and her heart **stopped**.

when and *while*

| He was running away **when** the bear attacked. |
| **While** he was running away, the bear attacked. |

- we use the simple past after *when*
- we use the past progressive after *while*

Present and Past Tenses

		present		
		simple		**progressive**
+		I / You walk He / She / It walks We / You / They walk		I 'm walking You 're walking He / She / It 's walking We / You / They 're walking
−		I / You don't walk He / She / It doesn't walk We / You / They don't walk		I 'm not walking You 're not walking He / She / It 's not walking We / You / They 're not walking
?		Do I / you walk? Does he / she / it walk? Do we / you / they walk?		Am I walking? Are you walking? Is he / she / it walking? Are we / you / they walking?

- we use the simple present for habits and daily routines
  She **brushes** her teeth before she goes to bed.
- we use the present progressive for an action that is happening at the moment of speaking
  What **are** you **doing** now?

	past	
	simple	**progressive**
	I / You walked He / She / It walked We / You / They walked	I was walking You were walking He / She / It was walking We / You / They were walking
	I / You didn't walk He / She / It didn't walk We / You / They didn't walk	I wasn't walking You weren't walking He / She / It wasn't walking We / You / They weren't walking
	Did I / you walk? Did he / she / it walk? Did we / you / they walk?	Was I walking? Were you walking? Was he / she / it walking? Were we / you / they walking?

- we use the simple past for a completed action or a completed sequence of actions in the past
  Last night I **had** dinner, **read** a book, and **went** to bed.
- we use the past progressive for an action that was in progress in the past
  I **was watching** TV at 10 o'clock last night.

PROGRESS CHECK

Name: _____
Class name / Period: _____
Teacher: _____
Date: _____

Prepositions

1 Complete the sentences with the words in the box.

> across   into   out of   under   up

a When John woke up, he climbed _____ his tent and ate breakfast.

b Then he walked to the river and dove _____ the water.

c While he was swimming _____ the river to the other side, it started to rain.

d When he reached the other side, he sheltered _____ a tree.

e When the rain stopped, he ran _____ a big hill.

-ed / -ing Adjectives

2 Complete the sentences with the correct form of the words in parentheses.

a They are very late. I am _____ (worry).

b The movie was really _____ (bore).

c Were you _____ (surprise) when you saw me?

d I'm reading a really _____ (interest) book.

e I can't find my smartphone. It's really _____ (annoy).

Review: Simple Past and Past Progressive

3 Complete the sentences with the correct form of the verbs in parentheses. Use the simple past or the past progressive.

a John _____ (not get up) early yesterday.

b At six o'clock yesterday I _____ (do) my homework.

c They _____ (not do) anything when I _____ (see) them.

d Kate _____ (meet) Kevin while she _____ (walk) to school.

4 Complete the questions using the simple past or the past progressive form of the verbs in parentheses.

a _____ (you / go) to a party last Saturday?

b What _____ (you / do) at 3am this morning?

c What _____ (you / do) last night?

d What _____ (your mother / do) when you _____ (wake up) this morning?

e What _____ (the other students / do) when your teacher _____ (arrive) today?

when and while

5 Complete the sentences with *when* or *while*.

a She was having dinner _____ Lucas called her.

b _____ you saw Liam, was he with Olivia?

c _____ she was reading, the lamp turned off.

d Her dad called _____ she was going home.

e I was really happy _____ my mom gave me a new laptop.

thirty-nine **39**

Present and Past Tenses

6 Write sentences using the simple present, the present progressive, the simple past, or the past progressive.

a Nicky / watch a movie / when / her friend / arrive.
_____
_____

b I / look for my friends / now.
_____
_____

c They / not usually eat / meat.
_____
_____

d While / they / swim / they / see a shark.
_____
_____

Grammar Buildup 2

1 **2** 3 4 5 6 7 8

7 Choose the correct options.

Todd Endris **a works / is working** in a laboratory, but he usually **b goes / is going** surfing in his free time. He loves **c surfing / surfed**! One day last summer, while he **d is surfing / was surfing** at Marina Beach, an enormous white shark **e attacked / was attacking** him. Todd **f hit / was hitting** the shark on the nose, but it **g didn't release / wasn't releasing** him. He **h got / was getting** desperate when suddenly six dolphins attacked the shark and Todd escaped. Two other surfers helped Todd get to the beach and **i call / called** an ambulance. Todd **j was / were** in the hospital for a long time, but he recovered. After a shark attack, most people are **k frightening / frightened** of surfing again, but not Todd. What **l does he do / is he doing** at the moment? Surfing, of course!

UNIT 2

VOCABULARY IN PICTURES

Prepositions

across | along | around | away from | down | into

out of | over | through | toward | under | up

-ed / -ing Adjectives

annoyed / annoying

bored / boring

excited / exciting

frightened / frightening

interested / interesting

surprised / surprising

tired / tiring

worried / worrying

forty-one 41

REVIEW 1

VOCABULARY

Start

1. He's an amazing **artist / lawyer**!

2. The train went **around / through** the tunnel.

7. He's running **out of / toward** the bus with a cup of coffee in his hand!

8. They're walking **around / along** the seashore.

9. He's the funniest **researcher / teacher** in the school.

10. He's the **mail carrier / firefighter** who brings all the correspondence to the neighborhood.

15. I'm **boring / bored**. Let's go to the movies.

16. Although the news from the doctor is very **worrying / worried**, I know he's going to recover soon.

17. I trust him to build my house he's an excellent **doctor / construction worker**.

18. The vehicles are going **up / around** the traffic circle.

42 forty-two

3 My sister and her friends are very **annoying / annoyed**! They broke my virtual reality headset.

4 I'm reading an e-book about the *aurora borealis*. It's really **interesting / interested**.

6 I'm in a **video conferencing / virtual reality** meeting right now.

5 We use **internet of things / cryptocurrency** to make our daily life easier.

11 They're getting **out of / into** the school bus.

12 We didn't like the movie. It was very **frightening / frightened**.

14 She is using **augmented reality / cloud storage service** to buy her clothes.

13 I'm **tiring / tired**. I think I'm going to bed.

19 She's the **lawyer / engineer** who is taking care of our court case.

20 A virtual reality headset makes your experience in **metaverse / artificial inteligence** games more immersive.

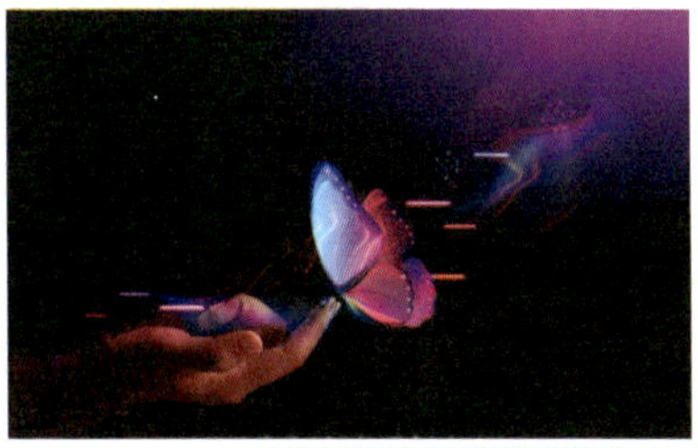

Finish

REVIEW 1

GRAMMAR

Simple Past

1 Complete with *was / wasn't* or *were / weren't*.

> It __was__ my parents' 25th wedding anniversary yesterday. My mom **a** _____ excited; it was just another normal day. There **b** _____ many letters in the mail that morning, but there **c** _____ a card from my dad. When my mom opened it, there **d** _____ two airline tickets to New York city in it. **e** _____ she excited then? Yes, she **f** _____. *Very* excited!

2 Complete the sentences with the simple past form of the verbs in parentheses.

I __sent__ (send) you a video conferencing invitation last night.

a Marc _____ (take) a picture of our avatars in metaverse.

b He finally _____ (use) his virtual reality headset!

c My mom _____ (work) at the school.

d I _____ (do) my homework after lunch.

3 Rewrite the sentences using the negative form.

You paid the inspector.
You didn't pay the inspector.

a They called the police officer.
_____

b I wrote a letter to the politician.
_____

c He met the researcher online.
_____

d They talked with the scientist and the technician.
_____
_____

4 Complete the simple past questions with the verbs in the box. Then write the correct short answers.

> ~~create~~   post   want   work

__Did__ he __create__ a video playlist at YouTube?
✗ _____ No, he didn't. _____

a _____ you _____ to be a firefighter?
✓ _____

b _____ they _____ at a social network?
✓ _____

c _____ your sister _____ as an artist?
✗ _____

Past Progressive

5 Complete the sentences with the past progressive form of the verbs in parentheses.

I __was__ __shopping__ (shop) a new e-book online yesterday.

a A school boy _____ _____ (use) virtual reality headset at the ICT class.

b He _____ _____ (not do) his homework on the computer.

c He _____ _____ (play) an online game.

d A man _____ _____ (wait) to use the computer for a video conferencing.

6 Write questions in the past progressive form. Then underline the correct words in the short answers.

you / live / in Paris / last year?
Were you living in Paris last year?

No, I **was** / **wasn't**.

a it / rain / at 6 o'clock?
_____
Yes, **he** / **it** was.

b Simon and Jen / work / as researchers?
_____
Yes, they **was** / **were**.

c mom and dad / using / streaming services?
_____
No, they **were** / **weren't**.

Simple Past and Past Progressive

7 Underline the correct options.

I saw the accident while I **walked** / **was walking** to school.

a A bus was coming along the road when a dog **ran** / **was running** in front of it.

b The driver **saw** / **was seeing** the dog and tried to avoid it.

c While the driver **tried** / **was trying** to avoid the dog, he drove into a tree.

d I quickly got my cell phone and **called** / **was calling** the emergency services.

8 Complete the sentences with the correct form of the verbs in parentheses. Use the simple past or the past progressive form.

Someone ___went___ into their room while they ___were sleeping___ (go / sleep).

a While Lucas _____, he _____ his leg (ski / break).

b I _____ home when I _____ a $50 bill (run / find).

c We _____ when the teacher _____ in (chat / come).

d Dad _____ a picture of us while we _____ (take / dive).

when and *while*

9 Complete the sentences with *when* or *while*.

I was surprised ___when___ I heard the news.

a They saw dolphins _____ they were sailing.

b We stayed inside _____ it was raining.

c _____ he saw the bear, he was walking in the forest.

d The dog was running toward me _____ it suddenly stopped.

Present and Past Tenses

10 Complete the sentences with the simple present or the present progressive form of the verbs in parentheses.

My dad ___gets___ (get) emails every day.

a We often _____ (go) out for a meal.

b I _____ (make) a curry right now.

c What _____ your mom _____ (do)?

d She _____ (eat) an apple now.

11 Complete the text with the verbs in parentheses. Use the simple past or the past progressive form.

I a _____ (do) my homework at 9 o'clock last night. I had to research about contemporary technology, but I b _____ (not know) what to write about. Then I heard a noise downstairs. I c _____ (switch) off my light and looked down. My sisters d _____ (use) virtual reality headsets at the living room. I e _____ (watch) them for ten minutes and then started doing my homework!

12 Number the sentences below according to the list of tenses.

1 simple present
2 present progressive
3 simple past (completed action)
4 simple past (sequence of actions)
5 past progressive (action in progress)
6 simple past and past progressive

[3] I slept badly last night.

a ☐ We were sleeping at 11 o'clock.

b ☐ Shhh! The baby's sleeping.

c ☐ The phone rang while I was sleeping.

d ☐ I sleep 8 hours a night.

e ☐ I got into bed and went to sleep.

DIGITAL LITERACY

Digital Natives *versus* Digital Immigrants

Generation Gap

Panel 1:
- May I come in?
- Sure, Daniel.

Panel 2:
- Are you all right, Ms. Clark?
- I'm fine. But I'm having trouble setting up this new VR headset.

Panel 3:
- I don't know where to find the instruction manual ...
- You don't need it. I found a video tutorial for setting up the headset. Let me help you.

Panel 4:
- Seconds later ...
- Ready!
- Oh, thank you, Daniel! ... And how can I help you?

Panel 5:
- I need a bit more time to finish my genetics assignment.
- Another extension?!

Panel 6:
- You know ... I have trouble concentrating ...
- Every generation has its quirks!

46 forty-six

1   Read and listen. Then match the questions with the answers.
    a Why is Daniel in Miss Clark's office?
    b Why is Miss Clark stressed?
    c Can Daniel configure the device?
    d Why can't Daniel finish his genetics assignment?

    ☐ Yes, he can. He watches an online video and quickly learns how to do it.
    ☐ He needs an extension for an assignment.
    ☐ He has difficulty concentrating.
    ☐ She can't configure an electronic device.

2   Write C for *Miss Clark* and D for *Daniel*.
    a ☐ To learn how to use a device, he or she looks for the instruction manual.
    b ☐ To learn how to use a device, he or she looks for shared knowledge on the web.
    c ☐ He or she multitasks: Looking for a video on the web while chatting with someone, for example.
    d ☐ He or she has concentration problems.

3   Join a classmate and discuss the following items. Then share your ideas with the class.
    a Read again: "Every generation has its quirks!" What did Miss Clark mean by that sentence?
    b Do you agree that Miss Clark and Daniel's abilities (or lack of abilities) are related to their age? Explain your ideas.

> **TIP**
>
> A **generation** is the set of people born and living at approximately the same time. You belong to one generation; your parents, to another; and your grandparents, to another.

4   Read the definitions of digital immigrants and digital natives in the table in activity 5. In the comic, which character is a digital native and which character is a digital immigrant?
    _____
    _____
    _____

5   Let's investigate, based on the informal poll below, how much the differences between digital natives and digital immigrants are present in our lives. Read the complete table and follow the topics.

Digital Immigrants Adopters of the web technologies	Me / My siblings or friends	My parents / Other adults
a Prefer to talk in person.	☐☐☐	☐☐☐
b Logical learners.	☐☐☐	☐☐☐
c Focus on one task at a time.	☐☐☐	☐☐☐
d Prefer to interact with one or few people rather than many.	☐☐☐	☐☐☐
e Get info from traditional new sites.	☐☐☐	☐☐☐
Digital Natives Born during or after the digital age	Me / My siblings or friends	My parents / Other adults
a Always online, attached to a phone or other device.	☐☐☐	☐☐☐
b Intuitive learners.	☐☐☐	☐☐☐
c Multitask and rapidly task-switch.	☐☐☐	☐☐☐
d Extremely social.	☐☐☐	☐☐☐
e Multimedia-oriented.	☐☐☐	☐☐☐

Source: DIGITAL Immigrants vs Digital Natives: Closing the Gap. *Unicheck*, Sep. 17, 2015. Available at: https://unicheck.com/blog/digital-immigrants-vs-digital-natives. Accessed on: Jul. 13, 2022.

   a You and your siblings (or friends, if you are an only child) will fill in the middle column of the table. Check (✓) if you have the behaviors and preferences indicated in each profile (digital immigrant and digital native). Then ask your parents and other adults around you to fill in the last column of the table.
   b The expectation is that you and your siblings or friends will give more answers compatible with the digital native profile, and your parents and other adults, with the digital immigrant profile.
   c When finished, share your results with the class. Did you see the expected result? Does only the younger generation have the characteristics of digital natives? Or are there enough exceptions for us to conclude that there aren't set features for each generation?

3
CELEBRATE!

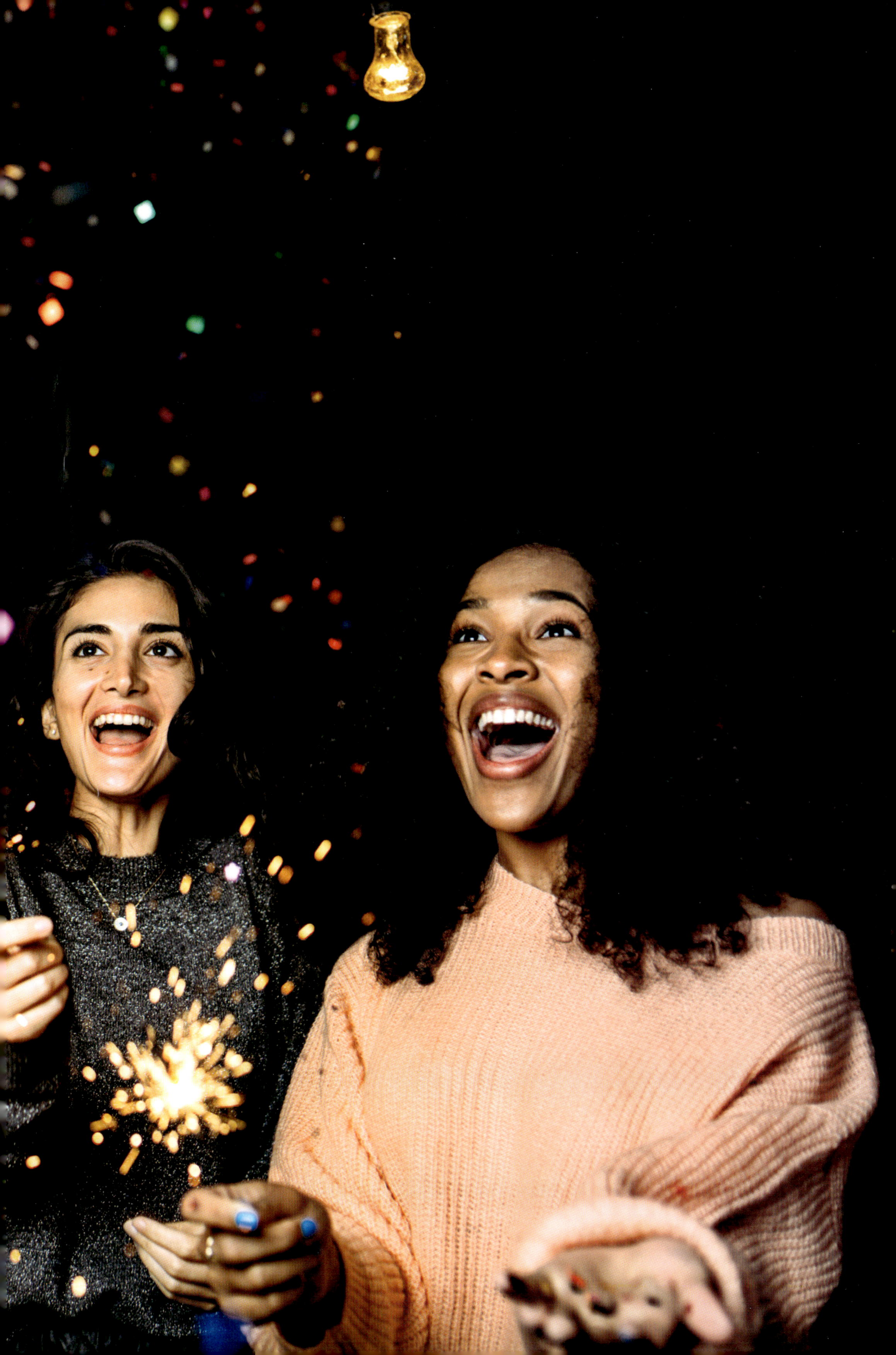

ABC VOCABULARY 1

Clothes and Accessories

1 Look at the words in the box. How do you say them in your language?

> boots   coat   dress   jacket   jeans
> pants   scarf   shirt   shorts   skirt
> sneakers   sweater   T-shirt

2 Listen to the words from activity 1 and repeat.

🔊 21

3 Match descriptions a-f to pictures 1-6.

- **a** I'm wearing a pair of jeans and a red coat. I'm having fun with my friends.
- **b** This is my brother and his wife at their wedding. My brother is wearing a special Scottish skirt called kilt.
- **c** This is my son on the beach. He's wearing a pair of shorts and a T-shirt.
- **d** This is New Year's Eve. It's December so we're wearing a coat, gloves, and a scarf.
- **e** This is my little brother's birthday party. He's wearing a multi-colored shirt.
- **f** It's Thanksgiving Day and my grandma is wearing her favorite sweater.

> **TIP**
> We often use *a pair of ...* with clothes:
> *a pair of pants, a pair of boots.*
> Remember that pants and boots are plural.
> *These are my favorite pants.*

4 Listen to Emily and Ben. What do they usually wear on special occasions?

🔊 22

_____
_____
_____
_____

5 👥 **INTERFACE** Work in pairs. Ask and answer questions about the clothes you wear. Use the words in the box or your own ideas.

> a party   a wedding
> New Year's Eve   school   the weekend

What do you usually wear to parties?

I usually wear a pair of jeans and a black T-shirt.

50 fifty

UNIT 3

READING 1

1 Skim the text and complete the headings with the words below.

a Gloves   b Skirts   c White

2 What genre does it illustrate?

a essay   b feature article

Dress Properly for these Celebrations!

Good Fun in _____

You can be sure it is going to be cold on New Year's Eve at Times Square, NY, so wear warm clothes! Coats, scarves, and boots are best. New Year's Eve has been celebrated at Times Square since 1904. Around one million locals and tourists gather near the New York Times' building to see a huge crystal ball descend from a tower during the countdown to midnight. And no one seems to complain about the freezing weather they have to endure to take part in this celebration. The organizers recommend many layers of clothing, a good hat, winter shoes, and gloves. It's a magical night of lights, fireworks, and friends, but anyone who doesn't dress warmly is going to freeze!

Not All Brides Wear _____

When Indian women get married, the traditional color isn't white but red, because this color is the symbol of new life. So, an Indian bride doesn't wear a white wedding dress, she wears a beautiful, long, red sari with red and gold jewelry and red henna on her hands.

Men in _____

If you're going to go to a *ceilidh*, you're going to need your dance clothes and comfortable shoes. *Ceilidhs* are traditional dances from Scotland and Ireland, and the music is fast and energetic. Everybody dances and has a good time, and *ceilidhs* are as popular as nightclubs. Girls wear what they want: jeans, skirts, or pants; boys wear kilts, shirts, and jackets. A kilt is similar to a skirt – it is a traditional Scottish outfit and it's perfect for dancing!

3 Read and listen to the text and answer the questions.

a Where do *ceilidhs* come from?

b What do girls wear to a *ceilidh*?

c What is the traditional color at an Indian wedding? Why?

d Why does the text recommend coats, hats, and scarves for New Year's Eve at Times Square?

e What do people gather to see?

READING STRATEGY

When you read a new word, read the context – the words around it – and try to guess the meaning.

4 Scan the text and underline words for these definitions.

a a traditional skirt from Scotland for men.

b a woman who is getting married.

c a red substance to color hair or skin.

d the counting backwards of numbers before an important event.

e colorful explosives, typical at celebrations.

5 **CLASS VOTE** Which is your favorite celebration?

GRAMMAR 1

be going to

1. Read the sentences. Underline the verb *be* and circle *going to* + verb.

   a You are going to need your dance shoes.
   b The music is going to be fast and energetic.
   c The Indian bride isn't going to wear white.
   d They are going to freeze on New Year's Eve.
   e We aren't going to take part in the Irish dance.

2. Look at the rules as to the use of *be going to* and complete the chart below.

   a The verb *be* in the simple present (am / is / are) is used before *going to*.
   b *going to* is followed by a verb in the base form.
   c The negative sentence is formed with the negative form of *be* (am not / isn't / aren't).

affirmative
I _____ going to wear a coat on New Year's Eve.
He / She / It is _____ be late.
We / You / They _____ going to take part in the dance next Saturday.
negative
I _____ going to be inside.
He / She / It _____ going to stop the dance.
We / You / They aren't going to _____ any songs.

3. Order the words to make sentences.

   a are / to / have / the beach / on / We / going / a party

   b I / to / wear / am / clothes / fancy / going / not

   c be / The music / to / going / great / is

   d sunny / is / going / not / It / to / a / be / day

   e am / sandwiches / I / take / going / cake / and / to

   f great time / You / to / have / are / going / a

TIP
Use time expressions with *be going to* to talk about future plans: *this August / weekend, next Tuesday / Christmas, on the weekend, tonight, tomorrow …*

4. Today is Monday and Sarah is at the museum on a school excursion. Look at her calendar and complete her plans for next days with the time expressions in the box.

MON 8	TUE 9	WED 10	THU 11
school excursion – museum	Jack and Ellie – movies	study science	science exam
FRI 12	**SAT 13**	**SUN 14**	**MON 15**
buy new dress	summer barbecue	study math	last exam – math! end of school ball

> next Monday   on Friday
> on the weekend   on Wednesday
> this Thursday   tomorrow

a Sarah's going to go to the movies with her friends _____.
b She's going to buy a new dress _____.
c She's going to study math _____.
d She's going to take her science exam _____.
e She's going to go to the school ball _____.
f She's going to study for the science exam _____.

52 fifty-two

UNIT 3

5 Look at the sentences below. Circle the verb *be*.

  a Are you going to wear a kilt? No, I am not.
  b Is it going to freeze during the night? Yes, it is.
  c Are we going to enjoy the night? Yes, we are.
  d Am I going to have a great time? Yes, you are.

6 Complete the chart. Note the use of *be going to* in questions and short answers.

questions and short answers	
_____ I going to have a great time?	Yes, you are. No, you _____.
_____ you going to wear a kilt?	Yes, I _____. No, I am not.
_____ it going to be a cold night?	Yes, it _____. No, it _____.
_____ he / she going to bring a friend?	Yes, he / she is. No, he / she _____.
_____ we / you / they going to be tired?	Yes, we / you / they _____. No, we / you / they _____.

7 Look at the sentences in the chart in activity 6 again. What is the correct order for questions?

  a subject + be + going to + verb + other words?
  b be + subject + going to + verb + other words?

8 Write questions using *be going to*.

Who / Sarah / go to the movies with?
Who is Sarah going to go to the movies with?

  a What / she / study on Wednesday?
     _____
  b What / she / buy this week?
     _____
  c What / she / visit today?
     _____
  d When / she / take / her last exam?
     _____
  e Where / they / have a barbecue?
     _____

9 Answer the questions in activity 8. Use Sarah's calendar in activity 4.

She's going to go to the movies with Jack and Ellie.

  a _____
  b _____
  c _____
  d _____
  e _____

10 **INTERFACE** Work in pairs. Ask and answer questions about your week.

> What are you going to do on Saturday?
>
> I'm going to play tennis with Anne.

➡ **GRAMMAR GUIDE** page 60

🎧 LISTENING

Costume Party

1 Listen to Emma, Ethan, and Conor talking about a costume party. Match the names to pictures 1-3.

2 Listen again and choose the correct words.

  a The party is on **Friday / Saturday**.
  b Emma **is / isn't** going to take her straw broom.
  c The party **is / isn't** going to be at Ethan's house.
  d Ethan's parrot **is / isn't** going to be real.
  e Conor is going to wear his **black / brown** boots.
  f Conor **is / isn't** going to wear a scarf.

🌐 Cultural fact

Costume parties became popular in the USA in the 19th century. Rich people dressed like historic European aristocrats and wore original accessories as a way to show off their wealth.

SPEAKING

A Birthday Party

Lisa is making a video call to Emma to invite her to her birthday party. Listen and complete the dialogue.

> Hi, Emma! How are you doing?

> Just fine, and you?

> Great! In fact, I **a** _____ a birthday party next Saturday. Do you want to come?

> Cool! What time **b** _____?

> Well, I'm having a barbecue, so I think 1pm is fine.

> **c** _____ all our friends from school?

> Not all of them, I guess, 'cause I can't spend too much money on it … But Jade and Josh **d** _____ … if that's what you wanted to know …

> Yeah, you know me quite well. Do you need help with anything?

> No, thanks! My parents **e** _____ everything!

> Well, Lisa, see you on Saturday, then … Oh, no, see you tomorrow at school!

FUNCTIONAL LANGUAGE

Extending and Accepting Invitations

I'm having …
I'm going to throw / give a … party …
Do you want to come?
Cool!
What time is it going to be?

Speaking Task

Create a dialogue between you and a classmate.

Step 1

Imagine it is your birthday and you are having a party. First, choose the party's theme. You can use the ideas below or your own.

Bowling Party
City Bowling Alley
7pm–9pm

Picnic in the Park
North Park
12:30pm–3:30pm

Step 2

Decide what to say.

I'm going to throw a … on …
Do you want to come? / Would you like to come?
I'm going to invite …
It is going to start at …

Think about what your classmate is going to say.

Cool!   *Who are you going to*
Thank you!   *invite?*
I'd love to!   *See you …*
What time is it going to start?

Step 3

Take turns practicing your dialogue.

UNIT 3

🌐 CULTURE

Birthday Traditions in Jamaica

Miss Lou

Jamaican children

'Appy birthday to yuh dear'

Birthday celebrations are always a festivity that warms the heart. Although people don't get a year younger, and, with time responsibilities pile up on their to-do list, they wish to be remembered on this special date.

In Jamaica, birthday celebrations are very similar to the ones in many western countries, with birthday cakes, birthday candles, sweets, and drinks. However, it's not just that – some traditions in Jamaica are a chapter unto themselves.

Jamaican birthdays come down to flouring! Regardless of age, tradition calls for the birthday boy or girl to be covered with flour, often topping it with some liquid to turn the dusting into cake batter. Friends either organize it during the party or as part of an ambush.

The traditional "Happy Birthday" song, which has only four short musical phrases and a single repetitive line of words, is sung in many languages all over the world. Jamaicans, however, have a special birthday song whose version was popularized by the Jamaican singer Miss Lou on a television show called "Ring Ding."

Jamaicans are very superstitious. A marriage superstition involves birthdays: if you want a happy, lifelong marriage, don't get married on your birthday as it may bring bad luck!

1 Read and listen. Then answer the questions below.

26 🔊

a In what ways are Jamaican birthday celebrations similar to the ones in many western countries?
_____
_____

b What birthday prank is played in Jamaica?
_____
_____

c Do Jamaicans sing the traditional birthday song? Explain.
_____
_____

d What superstition involves birthdays in Jamaica?
_____
_____

2 👥 **INTERFACE** How do people celebrate birthdays in your country? Are there any funny birthday pranks? Any superstitions? Share your ideas with your classmates.

VOCABULARY 2

Weather and Seasons

1 spring
2 summer
3 fall
4 winter

1 Look at the words in the box. How do you say them in your language?

> cloudy   cold   dry   hot   rainy   snowy
> stormy   sunny   warm   wet   windy

2 Listen to the words from activity 1 and repeat.
27))

3 Which words in activity 1 can you use to describe pictures 1-4?

1: It's warm, dry, and sunny.
2: _____
3: _____
4: _____

4 Choose the correct words.

a In the Arctic it's **cold / hot**.
b Summer in Mexico is usually **sunny / snowy**.
c People say that the weather in England is **dry / wet**.
d There was no rain last summer so the ground is very **dry / wet**.
e It's **warm / cold** tonight so we can sit outside and eat dinner.
f Last summer in Philadelphia was very **rainy / windy** – we used our umbrellas every day!

PRONUNCIATION

/s/

1 Listen and repeat.
28))

scarf	snowy
socks	sometimes
spring	stormy
summer	sunny

2 Listen and repeat.
29))
a It's sometimes sunny in spring and it's hot and stormy in summer.
b In winter you need a scarf, gloves, and thick socks because sometimes it's snowy.

5 **INTERFACE** Work in pairs. Ask and answer questions about your favorite season.

> What's your favorite season?

> It's autumn. It's windy and rainy, but I love the color of the trees.

> Yes, I agree, but I prefer …

56 fifty-six

UNIT 3

📖 READING 2

1 Skim the web page below. To whom is the cultural tip addressed?

   a To Chicago locals.
   b To tourists visiting Chicago.

2 Read and listen. How old is the Lollapalooza Festival?

🔊 30 _____

---

www.americantravel.com

Come to Lollapalooza ... But Bring Your Raincoat!

The Lollapalooza Chicago Festival has been happening every summer, around July / August, since the festival started in 1991! There are going to be over 170 acts this year – rock, pop, and dance music and more, including special circus, music, and theater acts for children. There are 400,000 tickets, but don't wait too long to buy them! The tickets are going to go on sale in March, but they usually sell all the tickets in one day. Your parents must send the organizers pictures of you and the other members of your family because all tickets are personal.

When you go to Chicago for the festival with your family, make sure to look for hotel, Airbnb, or other kinds of accommodation in advance.

Also, remember to take clothes for bad weather, like ponchos, boots, and especially raincoats, because it usually rains a lot and you must not enter the festival carrying an umbrella! But take your T-shirt and sunscreen too. You never know – it is summer after all!

🌐 Cultural fact

Lollapalooza was created by Perry Farrell, singer of the rock group Jane's Addiction. The festival's name comes from an archaic word meaning "extraordinarily impressive." Farrell claimed he chose the word after he heard it in a Three Stooges movie.

3 Read the text again. Then write T for *true* or F for *false*.

   a ☐ Lollapalooza is only a music festival.
   b ☐ The ticket demand is very high.
   c ☐ The festival does not allow children to enter.
   d ☐ Your parents must send the organizers a picture of you if you want a ticket.
   e ☐ It's a good idea to take clothes for good and bad weather.
   f ☐ The festival was created by a rock singer.

4 Are umbrellas allowed at Lollapalooza Chicago Festival? Why do you think this rule exists?

_____
_____
_____

5 👥 **INTERFACE** Has it ever rained while you were at an outdoor event? Would that be a problem for you? Why? Talk to a classmate.

> One time I was on a picnic and it rained like crazy.

> And what did you do?

> We stored the food in my parents' car and continued in the rain, playing with a ball. It was fun!

fifty-seven **57**

GRAMMAR 2

must / must not

1 Write O if the sentences express *obligation* and P if they express *prohibition*.

a ☐ You must not enter the festival carrying an umbrella.

b ☐ Your parents must send the organizers pictures of you and the other members of your family.

2 Look at the chart and check (✓) the correct statements and mark a cross (✗) on the incorrect ones.

affirmative	
I / You	**must** purchase the ticket through Lollapalooza.com.
He / She / It	**must** comply with the search policy.
We / You / They	**must** wear the wristband on the right hand.

negative	
I / You	**must not** carry backpacks.
He / She / It	**must not** bring professional cameras.
We / You / They	**must not** bring pets.

a ☐ *Must* and *must not* are used to express ability.

b ☐ The main verb (after *must / must not*) is without *to*.

c ☐ All pronouns (*I / you / he / she / it / we / you / they*) take *must* or *must not* + main verb.

3 Order the words to make sentences.

be / for / must not / late / You / school
<u>You must not be late for school.</u>

a you / send / must / of / parents / pictures / Your / organizers / the
_____

b do / People / must not / video recording / any / concert / at the
_____

c by an adult / Children / be accompanied / must
_____

d must not / with / items / enter / You / prohibited
_____

➡ **GRAMMAR GUIDE** page 60

CLIL

ART

Maori Music

In New Zealand, music is an important part of national culture. Wellington is the country's capital, and it is home to the New Zealand Symphony Orchestra, which sometimes tours overseas. The New Zealand School of Music is also based in Wellington.

New Zealand's most famous musical export is the opera singer Kiri Te Kanawa, who has appeared on stage around the world for five decades. She has performed with opera singer José Carreras and won many awards, including a Grammy in 1984. A soprano with a high singing voice, Kiri Te Kanawa is of Maori origin.

The Maoris are the native people of New Zealand and their traditional music uses special instruments, such as flutes made of animal bones – like the *nguru* flute –, trumpets made of seashells, and drums made with wood and the skin of sharks.

Some of New Zealand's biggest rock, hip-hop, and folk groups combine Maori music with European influences.

Annual Maori's presentation at the World Buskers Festival

Maori presentation with traditional instruments

Kiri Te Kanawa, opera singer

1 Read and listen. What are some of the special instruments the Maori people use to make music?

_____
_____

2 Choose the correct answers.

a Where is the New Zealand School of Music?
   1 Auckland
   2 Wellington
   3 Christchurch

b What type of singer is José Carreras?
   1 jazz
   2 pop
   3 opera

c When did Kiri Te Kanawa win a Grammy?
   1 1994
   2 1984
   3 1986

d What type of singer is Kiri Te Kanawa?
   1 contralto
   2 soprano
   3 mezzo-soprano

e Traditional Maori drums are made using …
   1 shark skin
   2 animal bones
   3 seashells

GRAMMAR GUIDE

be going to

affirmative	contracted form
I **am going to** wear	**'m going to** wear
You **are going to** wear	**'re going to** wear
He / She / It **is going to** wear	**'s going to** wear
We / You / They **are going to** wear	**'re going to** wear

- we use *be going to* to talk about plans or intentions in the future
- the form is subject + *be* + *going to* + verb
  I**'m going to** play tennis with my friends.
  You**'re going to** watch a movie.
  She**'s going to** buy some new clothes.

negative	contracted form
I **am not going to** play	**'m not going to** play
You **are not going to** play	**aren't going to** play
He / She / It **is not going to** play	**isn't going to** play
We / You / They **are not going to** play	**aren't going to** play

- we use *not* to form the negative
  I**'m not** (am not) **going to** wear sandals.
  He **isn't** (is not) **going to** have a party.
  They **aren't** (are not) **going to** visit their cousins.

questions and short answers	
Am I **going to** go?	
Yes, you **are**.	No, you **aren't**.
Are you **going to** go?	
Yes, I **am**.	No, I**'m not**.
Is he / she / it **going to** go?	
Yes, he / she / it **is**.	No, he / she / it **isn't**.
Are we / you / they **going to** go?	
Yes, we / you / they **are**.	No, we / you / they **aren't**.

- the word order is different in questions
  You **are going to** wear jeans.
  Are you **going to** wear jeans?

must / must not

affirmative
I / You **must** go
He / She / It **must** go
We / You / They **must** go

- we use *must* for obligation
  You **must** wear a uniform at this school.
- we use the same form for all subject pronouns

negative
I / You **must not** go
He / She / It **must not** go
We / You / They **must not** go

- we use *must not* for prohibition
  You **must not** take pictures.
- after *must* / *must not*, we use the verb without *to*
  You **must** bring your ticket.
  You **must not** litter.

PROGRESS CHECK

Name: _____
Class name / Period: _____
Teacher: _____
Date: _____

Clothes and Accessories

1 Complete the words with vowels.

a s c ____ r f
b s n ____ ____ k ____ r s
c c ____ ____ t
d j ____ c k ____ t
e T - s h ____ r t
f s k ____ r t

Weather and Seasons

2 Look at the map and choose the best words to complete the weather forecast.

50°F Washington, DC
68°F South Carolina
82°F Florida

It's June, I know, but in Washington DC today it's going to be **a** rainy / windy. With maximum temperatures of 50°F, it's going to be **b** warm / cold. In South Carolina it's going to be **c** warm / hot but **d** stormy / cloudy. In Florida it's going to be **e** cold / hot and **f** sunny / cloudy.

be going to

3 Order the words to make sentences or questions.

a friends / have / a beach party / My / are / to / going
_____
_____

b not / going / wear / I / am / to / that green dress
_____
_____

c make / you / a / Are / cake / to / going / chocolate ?
_____
_____

d is / Danny / dance / to / with / going / me
_____

must / must not

4 Complete the sentences with *must / must not*.

a You _____ bring glass bottles.
b You _____ only camp in designated areas.
c You _____ have a ticket.
d You _____ light fires.
e You _____ put your trash in the trash cans.

Grammar Buildup 3

1 2 **3** 4 5 6 7 8

5 Complete the dialogue with the correct form of the verbs in parentheses.

Emily Hi, Olivia! What **a** _____ you _____ (do) before I arrived?

Olivia Hi, Emily. I **b** _____ (put) these old school books in the basement.

Emily Oh, yes! It's the last day of school tomorrow.

Olivia I can't wait!

Emily **c** _____ you _____ (wear) your black dress tomorrow night?

Olivia No, of course I'm not. Why?

Emily It's the end of year school ball. **d** _____ you _____ (go)?

Olivia No, I'm not. I **e** _____ (go) last year and it **f** _____ (be) boring.

Emily Olivia, you always **g** _____ (go). We **h** _____ (have) a really good time last year. You **i** _____ (dance) with Jack, remember?

Olivia Yes, I remember. It **j** _____ (be) awful so I **k** _____ (not go) tomorrow.

Emily Oh, please! Connor, Eric, and I **l** _____ (meet) opposite the school at 7pm. Come with us!

UNIT 3

VOCABULARY IN PICTURES

Clothes and Accessories

boots

coat

dress

jacket

jeans

pants

scarf

shirt

shorts

skirt

sneakers

sweater

T-shirt

Weather and Seasons

fall

spring

summer

winter

cloudy

cold

dry

hot

rainy

snowy

stormy

sunny

warm

wet

windy

4

MAKE A DIFFERENCE

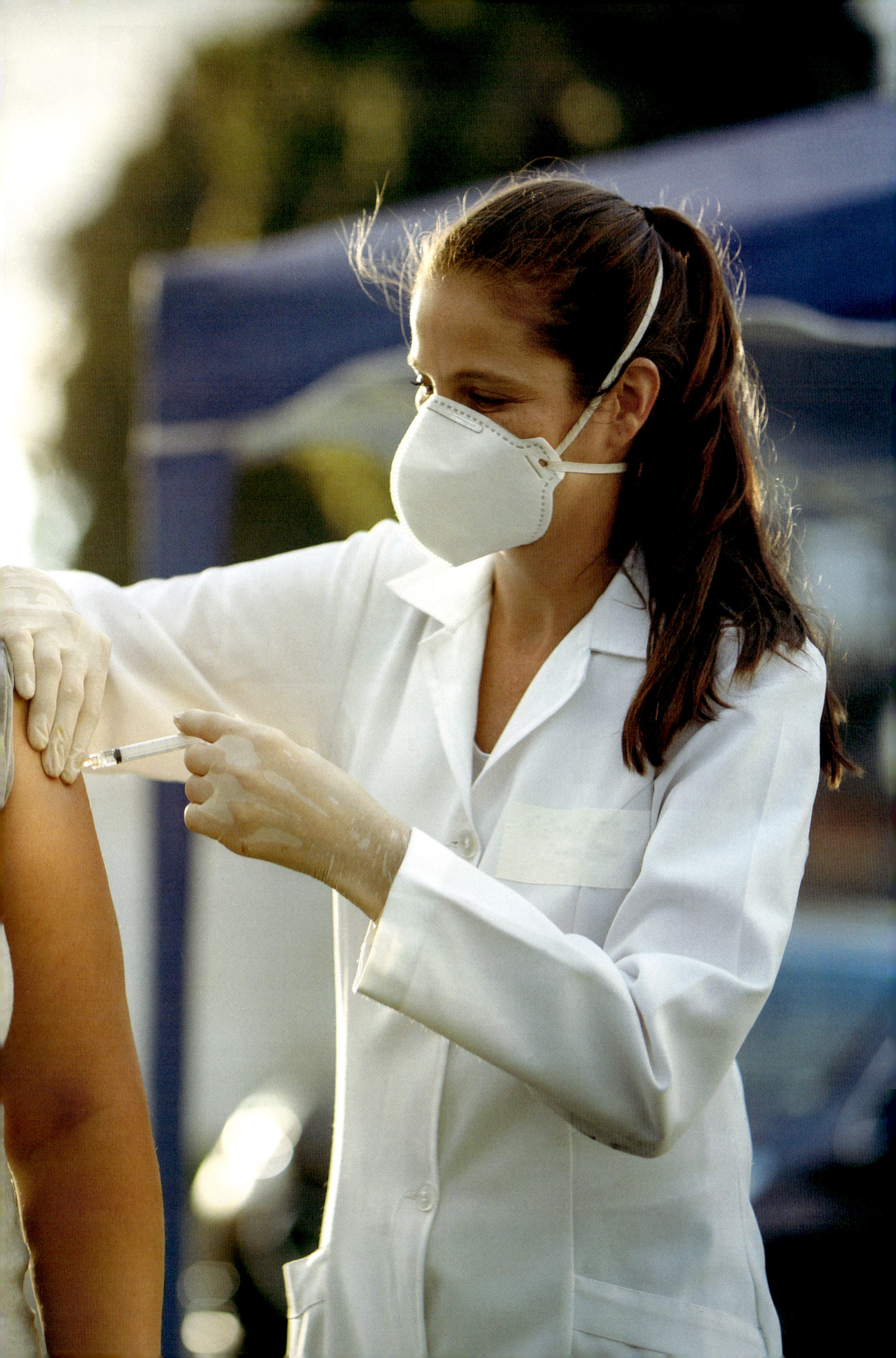

VOCABULARY 1

Jobs

1 Match pictures 1-6 with the jobs in the box. Mark an X next to the ones that aren't in the pictures.

actor	☐	psychologist	☐
athlete	☐	sign language interpreter	☐
conservation scientist	☐	social worker	☐
engineer	☐	surgeon	☐
historian	☐	teacher	☐
nurse	☐	vet	☐

2 Listen and repeat.
32))

3 Complete the definitions using job words from activity 1.

Performs in plays and movies? ___an actor___

a Plays professional sports? _____
b Studies and works with history? _____
c Designs and builds machines and roads? _____
d Cares for sick people? _____
e Practices surgery? _____
f Cares for animals? _____

4 **INTERFACE** Work in pairs. Reflect on the importance and contribution of the jobs in activity 1.

> What do you think about the health and science area jobs?

> I think they're really important, because scientists create vaccines and medication, for example.

66 sixty-six

UNIT 4

WORLD WATER DAY
AN INTERNATIONAL DAY OF ACTION

Almost 1 billion people in the world don't have clean water to drink.
2.5 million people don't have access to a toilet.
Every day, 24,000 children under the age of 5 die because of unsafe water.
Many children can't go to school because they need to walk for hours to get water for their family.

March 22 is World Water Day, when there are events around the world focusing on the water crisis. So what should we do on World Water Day?

Stand in a toilet queue*

Jamie Cranks and his friends are from Vancouver, Canada. March 22 isn't going to be a normal school day for them because they're going to stand in an unusual queue. Their teacher is going to join them too! In fact, people in about 80 countries are going to work together to form the world's longest toilet queue.

Donate your Facebook or Twitter status.

Amy, her friends, and thousands of other people are going to donate their Facebook and Twitter status to Water.org from March 21 to 26. When Hollywood actor Matt Damon and engineer Gary White created the organization, they had a clear objective: Everyone should have access to clean water to drink. Water.org works with local partners to help individuals and communities to meet their own water and sanitation needs. On World Water Day, Water.org is inviting people to donate their Facebook and Twitter statuses to tell millions about the water crisis.

American engineer Gary White and American actor Matt Damon, co-founders of Water.org

TIP
*queue: a line of people waiting in a store or similar place

📖 READING 1

1 Read and listen to the text above. What do the numbers below refer to?

a 1 billion
b 2.5 million
c 24,000
d 5
e 22
f 80

2 What text genre is this?

a ☐ a commercial ad.
b ☐ an institutional ad.

3 Read the text again. Then write T for *true* or F for *false*.

a ☐ Some people travel long distances to find water.
b ☐ World Water Day is celebrated in the UK only.
c ☐ Jamie Cranks is going to queue on March 22.
d ☐ Water.org is going to use Amy's Facebook status.
e ☐ Water.org sends engineers and mechanics from Hollywood to developing countries.

4 Answer the questions.

a What happens on World Water Day?

b What world record do Jamie and his friends hope to break?

c What does Water.org do?

d What is Water.org going to do on World Water Day?

TIP
Learn to recognize prefixes like *un-*. They can help you guess the meaning of a word.

5 Match the words below with their meaning.

a unclear   ☐ not needed
b unsafe   ☐ dangerous
c unnecessary   ☐ not obvious
d unusual   ☐ not normal, not ordinary

6 ✋ **CLASS VOTE** Which World Water Day idea do you prefer?

sixty-seven **67**

🔑 GRAMMAR 1

should (Affirmative and Negative)

1. Read the following sentences. Write G for *good* if the recommendation / suggestion given is good and B for *bad* if it is not appropriate.

   a ☐ Everyone should have access to clean water to drink.
   b ☐ Saving water shouldn't be a real concern.
   c ☐ People shouldn't use less water outdoors.
   d ☐ People should consider when and how much water is needed.
   e ☐ Reusing and recycling water should be considered.

2. Complete the rules below with *should* or *shouldn't*.

   a _____ is used to make recommendations and give advice. In a sentence, it gives the meaning of "It is a good idea."
   b _____ is the negative form and means that you *aren't recommending or advising* something: "It's NOT a good idea."
   c The sentence structure is: subject + _____ (or _____) + base form of the verb.

3. Complete the chart with *should* or *shouldn't*.

affirmative	
I / You	_____ save water.
He / She / It	_____ consider saving water.
We / You / They	_____ recycle water.
negative	
I / You	_____ waste water.
He / She / It	_____ be left out.
We / You / They	_____ drink unsafe water.

4. Complete the information about saving water at home with *should* or *shouldn't*.

   a You _____ turn off the faucet when you brush your teeth.
   b You _____ take long showers.
   c You _____ fix a dripping faucet.
   d You _____ water your garden with a hose.
   e You _____ run washing machines when they are not full.

5. Read the situations below and give people some advice / recommendation.

   a You are walking down a street and you see two kids throwing trash on the sidewalk.
   _____
   _____
   _____
   _____

   b Your neighbor is watering his plants with a hose. He's been doing it for two hours!
   _____
   _____
   _____
   _____

   c Your little brother is flushing the toilet nonstop!
   _____
   _____
   _____
   _____

   d Your friend is doing the dishes under constantly flowing water.
   _____
   _____
   _____
   _____

UNIT 4

6 Look at the pictures below. Say what people should or shouldn't do. Use the clues to complete the sentences.

a People (✗) _____.

b People (✓) _____ in parks.

c Everybody (✓) _____ when leaving a place.

d People (✗) _____.

➡ **GRAMMAR GUIDE** page 76

🎧 LISTENING

Heroes

1 You are going to listen to Emma, Rosie, and Liam talking about their heroes. First, look at the pictures. What do you think these people do?

_____
_____

2 Listen and match the person with their hero.
34 🔊

a Emma
b Rosie
c Liam

☐ Charlotte
☐ Mr. Benson
☐ Sky Brown

3 Listen again and choose the correct options.
34 🔊

a Sky Brown won the bronze medal for skateboarding in **2018 / 2020**.

b Sky Brown also inspires **her friends / young girls**.

c Charlotte's going to work in a camp for **700 / 100,000** people.

d Charlotte's going to work with **children / families**.

e Mr. Benson **is / isn't** going to retire next year.

f Mr. Benson is the **math / science** teacher.

4 Listen again and answer the questions.
34 🔊

a How old was Sky Brown when she competed in the Olympics?
_____

b Where is Charlotte going to work?
_____

c What other job does Mr. Benson have?
_____

5 Who is your hero? Why?
_____
_____

sixty-nine **69**

SPEAKING

A Class Presentation

1 Read and listen to the class presentation. What is it about? Check (✓) all that apply.

🔊 35

a ☐ Raise awareness of an important issue.

b ☐ Present the result of a scientific experiment.

c ☐ Inspire their classmates to take action.

Emily: Hello, class! As you probably know, today is World Water Day. This event is celebrated every March 22 by the United Nations to remind people how essential water is.

Ava: Water is essential for sure, not only to put an end to thirst and protect health, but also for supporting economic, social, and human development.

Leah: On this date, we'd like to talk to you about the need to tackle water and sanitation issues. We must consider the problem of pollution. Contaminated water puts people at risk of contracting lots of diseases and dying. In fact, unsafe water, poor sanitation, and bad hygiene cause thousands of deaths every year around the world.

Emily: Next, we need to think about the inequality of access to water services, particularly in developing countries. The lack of quality water makes social inequality worse. For example, children who live in neighborhoods without sewers get sick more often and miss school more.

Ava: For all these reasons, World Water Day should be an important event in the school calendar. We, students, must remind our parents of the importance of demanding an abundance of quality water. And that goes not only for our neighborhood, but for all cities, in all countries. Talk to your parents or guardians about this.

Leah: Thanks for your attention. Does anyone have any questions or would like to make a comment?

2 Complete with *Emily*, *Leah*, or *Ava*. Then number the sentences in the correct order.

a ☐ _____ thanks the audience and invites questions or comments.

b ☐ _____ talks about the damage caused by water pollution.

c ☐ _____ highlights the importance of water in our lives.

d ☐ 1 ___Emily___ greets the audience and explains what World Water Day is about.

e ☐ _____ recommends her classmates to talk about the importance of the date.

f ☐ _____ talks about the relationship between unequal access to water services and social inequality.

FUNCTIONAL LANGUAGE

Giving a Class Presentation

We'd like to talk about ...
The focus of this presentation is ...
Firstly / Next / Finally ...
For all these reasons ...
To sum up ...

Speaking Task

Plan a class presentation with your classmates.

Step 1

Work with one or two partners. Choose one of the following events or use an idea of your own.

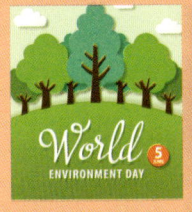

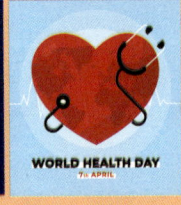

Step 2

Search for information about the event.

Who created it?
For what purpose?
What are the main issues discussed on that date?
What actions can be taken to address them?

Distribute the parts of the presentation among yourselves. Plan the introduction, the main topics, and the conclusion.

Join your group and practice the presentation.

Step 3

Give your presentation to the class. Then discuss with your classmates.
What did you like most about each presentation? Why?
What could be improved in an upcoming presentation?

UNIT 4

🌐 CULTURE

Trinidad and Tobago and Its Cultural Relationship with the Ocean

Trinidad and Tobago, a two-island nation in the southern Caribbean, is home to nearly 1.4 million people whose existence is tied to the sea. Trinidadians ("Trinis," as citizens proudly call themselves) and Tobagonians say they are blessed with a particular phenomenon in that their country consists of 15 times more ocean than land area. They firmly believe they have to pay attention to the marine and coastal environments, home to fish, sharks, turtles, coral reefs, and numerous marine organisms.

Trinidadians understand that oceans are part of what it means to be a Trini. There is a traditional ritual when a baby is born: At a specific time, babies are taken to the beach to dip their feet in the saltwater, so that they can grow up healthy. When you are sick or there is something wrong with you, such as an upset stomach, you should go to the beach to drink some of the salt water.

Oceans play an essential role in human well-being, producing half of the oxygen for life on the planet. Therefore, Trinidadians and Tobagonians are aware of the importance of sustainable development, which includes action on ocean-related issues such as reducing plastic pollution and addressing the impact of climate change. Protecting the ocean to protect humanity is their goal.

1 Read and listen to the information. Then check (✓) the correct options below.

36 🔊

a Trinidad and Tobago …
   ☐ has an intimate relationship with the sea.
   ☐ consists of one island in the southern Caribbean.

b Trinis feel …
   ☐ the marine and coastal environments aren't of vital importance.
   ☐ they are blessed by living in a region where the ocean covers more area than the land.

c When babies are born …
   ☐ they are taken to the sea to dip their feet in the saltwater.
   ☐ they are blessed by a local priest.

d Trinis believe …
   ☐ boiling and bathing in seawater can heal many diseases.
   ☐ drinking sea water helps heal an upset stomach.

e Trinidadians and Tobagonians …
   ☐ know the importance of sustainable development.
   ☐ think they don't need to worry about actions on ocean-related issues.

2 In your country, are there any cultural traditions related to nature? Describe it / one of them and its impact on people's lives.

_____

_____

ABC VOCABULARY 2

Health Problems

1 Read the words in the box. Which words can you use to describe pictures a-d?

broken arm ☐	cut ☐	insect bite ☐	stomachache ☐
cold ☐	earache ☐	sick ☐	temperature ☐
cough ☐	headache ☐	sore throat ☐	

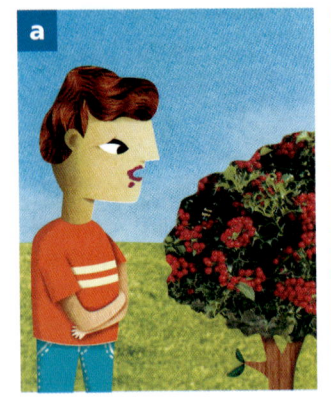

2 Listen and repeat.

37)))

3 Choose the correct options.

a A **headache / stomachache** is when you have a pain in your head.
b He went outside without a coat in January and now he has **a cold / an insect bite**.
c She has a **sore throat / stomachache** because she ate her dinner very quickly.
d I was talking all day yesterday and now I have **a sore throat / a broken arm**.
e When you eat some spoiled food, you can get **sick / an earache**.
f The baby is now cured of the infection but still has a **cut / temperature**.

4 Answer the questions. Use the words in the box.

> drink water   have a cough drop   lie down
> put on a bandage   take an aspirin

What do you do when you have …

… a headache? <u>I take an aspirin and I lie down.</u>

a … a sore throat? _____
b … a cough? _____
c … a cut? _____
d … a temperature? _____

72 seventy-two

UNIT 4

📖 READING 2

1 Read and listen to the interview. Then answer: What does John Martin do in his free time?

_____
_____

Mountain Rescue!

John Martin works for the rescue service in the Yosemite National Park.

Q: John, is this your only job?
A: No, I'm an engineer, but in my free time I'm a volunteer for the rescue service.

Q: What are the most common problems?
A: A very common problem is exhaustion. If someone in your group looks tired, you should all rest. You should also carry high-energy food, like chocolate.

Q: And what should I do if someone has a broken leg or arm? Should I move him or her?
A: No, you shouldn't move him or her. You should call for help.

Q: Who should I contact?
A: You should call 911 to speak to the police. While you wait, you should keep the person warm.

Q: What about for minor things like insect bites?
A: Use cold water or a special cream, but if the person has a temperature you should go to the hospital.

2 Read the text again. Then write T for *true* or F for *false*.

- **a** ☐ John Martin's only job is to work as a volunteer for the rescue service.
- **b** ☐ John Martin mentions a broken leg or arm as one of the most common problems.
- **c** ☐ John Martin recommends calling 911 to ask for help.
- **d** ☐ John Martin says that anyone with an insect bite should go to the hospital.

3 What is John Martin's advice for these situations?

a Someone feels tired.
_____

b Someone has a broken leg.
_____

c You need to speak to the police.
_____

d Someone has an insect bite.
_____

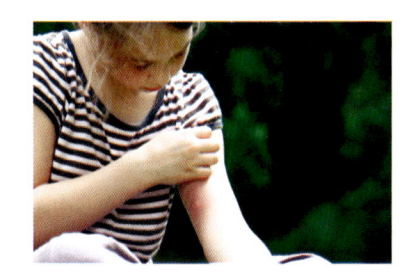

e Someone has a temperature.
_____

seventy-three **73**

GRAMMAR 2

should (Questions and Short Answers)

1 Read the questions below and choose the best answer for each one of them.

a Should you cover your mouth when you cough?
☐ Yes, we should. ☐ No, we shouldn't.

b Mark has broken his leg. Should he call for help?
☐ Yes, he should. ☐ No, he shouldn't.

c The kids are sick. Should they go swimming?
☐ Yes, they should. ☐ No, they shouldn't.

d Jane has a sore throat and a cough. Should she go to the hospital?
☐ Yes, she should. ☐ No, she shouldn't.

2 Complete the rules below with the words in the box.

affirmative   questions   short answers

a In _____, *should* comes before the subject.

b In _____, use *should* (_____) and *shouldn't* (negative).

3 Refer to activities 1 and 2 and complete the chart below.

questions and short answers
_____ I / you go to the hospital?
Yes, I / you _____.
No, I / you _____.
_____ he / she / it move the person?
Yes, he / she / it _____.
No, he / she / it _____.
_____ we / you / they go swimming?
Yes, we / you / they _____.
No, we / you / they _____.

4 Write complete questions.

I have a terrible cold. stay at home / go to school?
Should I stay at home or should I go to school?

a I always feel terrible on buses. sit at the front / sit at the back?
_____

b It's my mom's birthday. buy her a present / make her dinner?
_____

c My friends want to learn a new language. study Chinese / study German?
_____

d We want to try a new activity. go paintballing / go karting?
_____

5 Read the information below. Then answer the questions that follow.

There are several things you can do to relieve pain in case of insect bites or stings. Here are a few:
- Don't panic!
- Apply an ice pack to a bite or sting for 15 to 20 minutes once an hour for the first 6 hours.
- Elevate the area of the bite or sting to decrease swelling.
- Do not use any cream on children younger than age 2 without a medical's prescription.

In case of an insect bite or sting …

a Should we panic?
_____

b Should people apply an ice pack to the sting for 15 to 20 minutes once an hour for the first 6 hours?
_____

c Should we elevate the area of the bite or sting to decrease swelling?
_____

d Should adults use a cream on children younger than age 2 without a medical's prescription?
_____

➡ **GRAMMAR GUIDE** page 76

WRITING

An Account for a Local Newspaper

① EXPLORING THE CONTEXT

1 Skim the texts on page 75. Where do the likely readers of Haley and Matt's accounts live?
_____

2 Read and listen to the texts on page 75. Who decided to talk about a member of his or her family?
_____

39 🔊

UNIT 4

The Springwall News
Springwall's Oldest Newspaper   Sunday, May 13, 2022
WWW.SPRINGWALLNEWS.COM

LOCAL HEROES

Tell us about your hero. This could be a member of your family, a friend, or someone who works in our town.

A few years ago, my grandmother was in Northbridge Hospital for several weeks. The doctors told her, "You should change your habits!" She began to eat a healthier diet and she also started to play sports.

Next week she's going to run a half marathon to raise money for the hospital. She's also going to work at the hospital as a volunteer. She's going to talk to patients who don't usually have visitors. What a hero!

Haley, 13.

·················

I'm going to nominate our vet, Ms. Rodgers. Last week, our dog Rudy jumped off our balcony. He had a broken leg and a terrible cut on his face too. Ms. Rodgers was very patient, and she was also very kind. Rudy's going to be fine. Thank you, Ms. Rodgers!

Matt, 11.

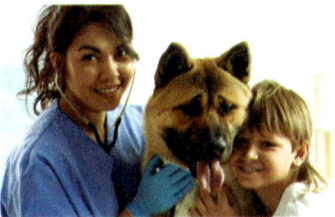

3 Why do Haley and Matt consider these people heroes? Underline the sentences that show the reasons.

4 What adjectives does Matt use to describe Ms. Rodgers?

_____

5 Haley doesn't use adjectives to describe her grandmother. Which of these could she use?

  a ☐ stubborn
  b ☐ lazy
  c ☐ persistent

2 PLANNING

Write an account about your local hero. Make notes under three headings:
  a Who is your hero?
  b Why is he or she your hero?
  c What is he or she going to do next?

LANGUAGE FOCUS

also and too

Use *also* and *too* to add new information and make your writing more interesting.

She **also** started to play sports.
He had a terrible cut on his face **too**.

1 Look at the sentences above. Where do *too* and *also* go in the sentence?

_____
_____

2 Rewrite the sentences including the words in parentheses.
  a We should run a marathon. We should climb Ben Nevis. (also)

  _____
  _____

  b They're going to look after children. They're going to look after animals. (too)

  _____
  _____

3 WRITING

Write a first draft. Use your notes from Step 2 and the accounts on the previous page to help you. Try to include *also* and *too*.

4 CHECKING & EDITING

1 Ask a classmate to read your account.
  • Can you identify who my hero is and why I admire him or her?
  • Were the verb tenses used correctly?

2 Use your classmate's suggestions to prepare the final version of your text. If possible, include a picture of you and your hero.

5 SHARING

Organize a "Local Heroes" panel in the classroom. Read the accounts of your classmates and exchange ideas:
  a Are any hero choices surprising or interesting?
  b What types of people are the most admired?

GRAMMAR GUIDE

should (Affirmative and Negative)

	affirmative and negative	
+	I / You / He / She / It We / You / They	should go.
–	I / You / He / She / It We / You / They	shouldn't go.

should (Questions and Short Answers)

questions and short answers	
Should I / you **go**?	
Yes, I / you **should**.	No, I / you **shouldn't**.
Should he / she / it **go**?	
Yes, he / she / it **should**.	No, he / she / it **shouldn't**.
Should we / you / they **go**?	
Yes, we / you / they **should**.	No, we / you / they **shouldn't**.

- we use *should* and *shouldn't* to ask for and give advice and recommendations
  You **should** go to the hospital.
  You **shouldn't** go to the party.

- the form is the same for all subject pronouns
  He **should** stop and rest.
  We **shouldn't** move.

76 seventy-six

PROGRESS CHECK

Name: _____
Class name / Period: _____
Teacher: _____
Date: _____

Jobs

1 Identify the jobs.

a_____

e_____

h_____

n_____

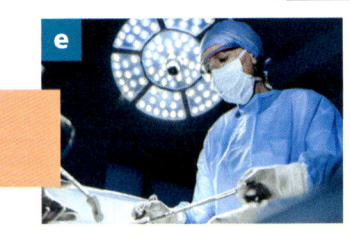

s_____

v_____

Health Problems

2 Match the symptoms with the cures.

a I have a sore throat.
b I have a temperature.
c He has a broken leg.
d I have a mosquito bite.
e I have a horrible cut.

☐ Here's some cream.
☐ Have a cough drop!
☐ Would you like a bandage?
☐ You should take an aspirin.
☐ You shouldn't move him.

should (Affirmative and Negative)

3 Complete the sentences with *should* or *shouldn't*.

a I want to be a teacher, but I'm not very good at teaching.

You _____ (✗) worry about teaching. You _____ (✓) study teaching skills.

b My sister wants to play soccer, but her friends say hockey is better.

She _____ (✓) listen to her friends. She _____ (✗) play soccer.

c My friends are going to climb a mountain.

They _____ (✗) continue if they are tired. They _____ (✓) wear comfortable shoes.

d I have a headache and a temperature, but I want to meet my friends.

You _____ (✓) lie down.
You _____ (✗) meet your friends.

seventy-seven **77**

should (Questions and Short Answers)

4 Read the questions and check (✓) the correct options.

a Should I go to the beach with a broken arm?
☐ Yes, you should.
☐ No, you shouldn't.

b My mom has broken her leg. Should I call the hospital?
☐ Yes, you should.
☐ No, you shouldn't.

c My dream is acting. Should I study to be an actor?
☐ Yes, you should.
☐ No, you shouldn't.

d My dad has an insect bite. Should he use hot water?
☐ Yes, he should.
☐ No, he shouldn't.

Grammar Buildup 4

| 1 | 2 | 3 | 4 | 5 | 6 | 7 | 8 |

5 Complete the dialogue with the correct form of the verbs in parentheses.

Dad You **a** _____ (look) awful. What **b** _____ (be) wrong?

Lou I **c** _____ (run) home when I **d** _____ (fall).

Dad Oh dear. **e** _____ it _____ (hurt)?

Lou Yes, and I **f** _____ (play) soccer tomorrow. What should I **g** _____ (do)?

Dad You should **h** _____ (put) some ice on it. Can you **i** _____ (move) it?

Lou No, not really. It **j** _____ (feel) really painful.

Dad Let's **k** _____ (call) to the hospital.

Lou OK. **l** _____ you _____ (have) the number?

Dad Yes, here you go.

Lou Thanks, dad.

UNIT 4

A VOCABULARY IN PICTURES

Jobs

actor  — athlete  — conservation scientist  — engineer

historian  — nurse  — psychologist  — sign language interpreter

social worker 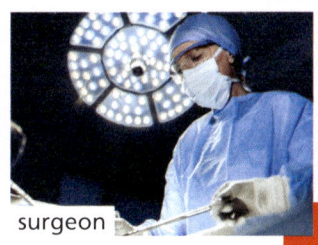 — surgeon  — teacher  — vet

Health Problems

broken arm  — cold  — cough 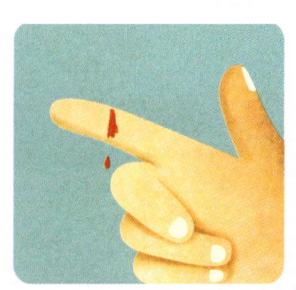 — cut

earache  — headache  — insect bite  — sick

sore throat  — stomachache  — temperature

seventy-nine 79

REVIEW 2

VOCABULARY

1. As an …, I'm going to be able to perform in theaters all over the world.
2. I bought new … for me, it feels like I'm stepping on clouds.
3. I need a sweater, the weather today feels …
4. I need some drops, this … is terrible.
5. Could you give me some bandage? I have a … on my finger.
6. The soil is extremely …
7. A pain in your head is a …
8. I want to be a … because I love studying history in school.
9. I'm sweating, it feels so … today.
10. Should I buy a new … or a sweater?

11 I usually wear a pair of … and a white T-shirt.

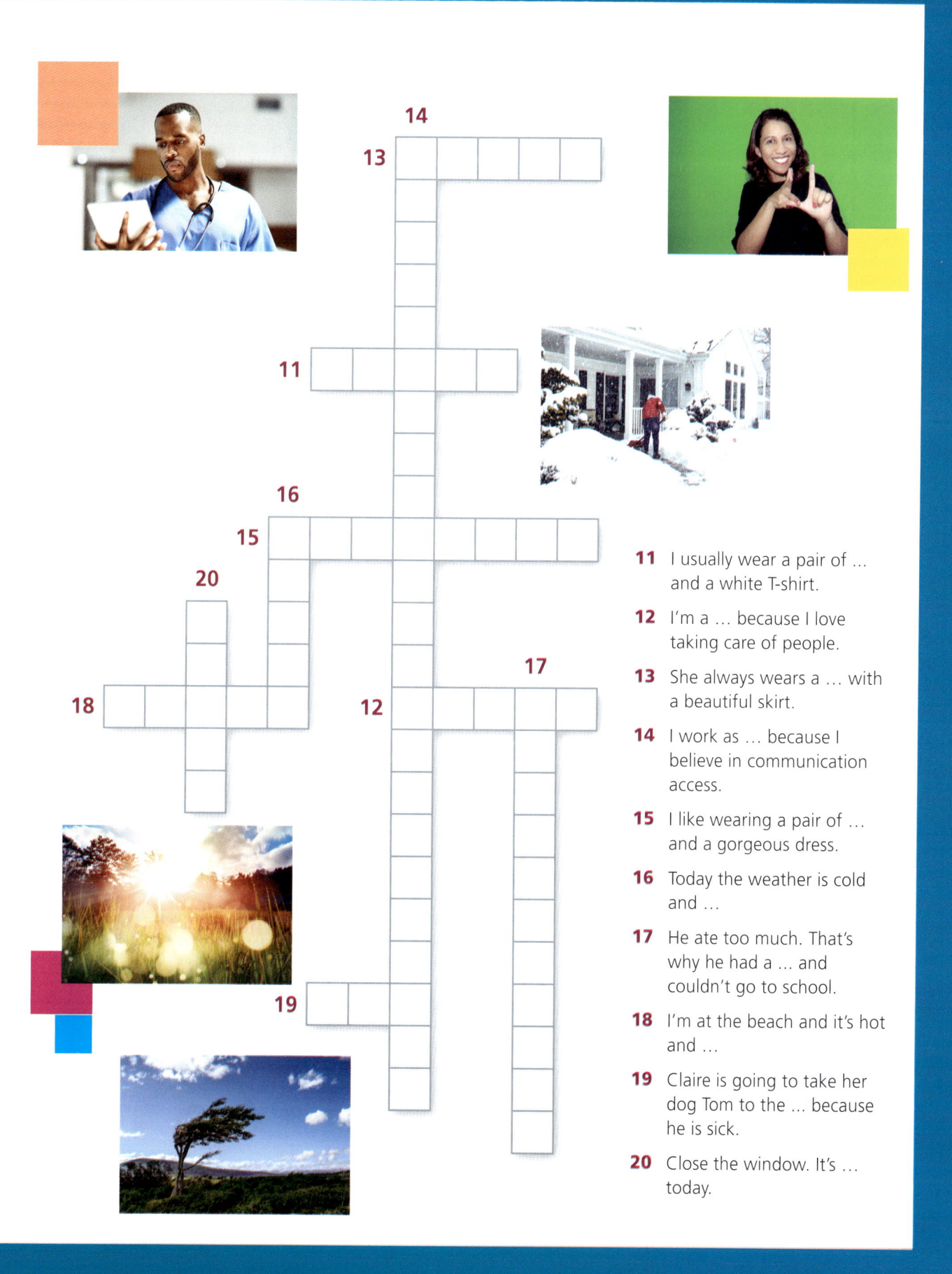

12 I'm a … because I love taking care of people.

13 She always wears a … with a beautiful skirt.

14 I work as … because I believe in communication access.

15 I like wearing a pair of … and a gorgeous dress.

16 Today the weather is cold and …

17 He ate too much. That's why he had a … and couldn't go to school.

18 I'm at the beach and it's hot and …

19 Claire is going to take her dog Tom to the … because he is sick.

20 Close the window. It's … today.

REVIEW 2

GRAMMAR

be going to

1 Write affirmative sentences with *be going to*.

My dad / arrive home late
My dad is going to arrive home late.

a We / live in Scotland

b My football team / win the game

c It / be cloudy

d They / wear sneakers

e I / study for my exams

f My classmates / have a party

2 Rewrite the sentences in the negative form.

I'm going to visit my grandmother.
I'm not going to visit my grandmother.

a They're going to read a book.

b Harry's going to dance at the school ball.

c We're going to have a terrible time.

d Eva's going to walk to school.

e You're going to call your cousin.

3 Complete the questions with *be going to* and the verbs in the box.

| drink | fly | hit | meet |
| ~~play~~ | sunbathe | watch | |

Are you *going to play* basketball later?

a _____ your mom _____ orange juice for breakfast?

b _____ your friends _____ TV tonight?

c _____ your uncle _____ the airplane?

d _____ we _____ on the beach?

e _____ you _____ the ball?

f _____ I _____ you in front of the park?

4 Write short answers for the questions in activity 3.

✓ *Yes, I am.*

a ✗ _____
b ✗ _____
c ✓ _____
d ✓ _____
e ✓ _____
f ✗ _____

must / must not

5 Complete the sentences with *must* or *must not*.

You *must not* play basketball inside the classroom.

a We _____ speak English in our French class.

b I _____ do my homework every day.

c They _____ talk loudly in the library.

d Olympic athletes _____ train every day.

e You _____ take a shower before you enter the swimming pool.

f We _____ write on our desks.

should (Affirmative and Negative)

6 Complete the how-to list using *should* or *shouldn't*.

www.healthlifetraining.com

What you _should_ **or** _shouldn't_ **do when you hurt yourself while training**

❶ First of all, you **a** _____ panic! That can only make things worse. You **b** _____ take a deep breath and face the situation.

❷ If you're on the street or at any unsafe place, you **c** _____ first check if you can walk to move to a safe place.

❸ You **d** _____ ask for help to leave the unsafe spot in case you have any difficulties walking.

❹ Don't try to move the injured body part on your own. You **e** _____ call your local emergency services.

❺ After seeing the doctor, you **f** _____ follow his or her instructions carefully to heal soon!

7 Complete the sentences with *should* or *shouldn't*.

I feel tired and I have a headache. I think I _should_ lie down.

a Henry has a terrible stomachache. He _____ eat any more cake.

b It's my friend's birthday. I _____ call her.

c That old woman wants to cross the road. We _____ help her.

d The party starts at 7:30pm. You _____ be late.

e They use the laptop every day. They _____ sell it.

f I can't understand you. You _____ speak more slowly.

should (Questions and Short Answers)

8 Order the words to make questions.

I / a cream / use / Should ?
Should I use a cream?

a study / my brother / Russian / Should ?
_____

b buy / Should / new sneakers / I ?
_____

c we / fly / Should / to Galicia ?
_____

d money / they / Should / borrow ?
_____

e a surgeon / Rachel / be / Should ?
_____

f this water / Should / we / drink ?
_____

9 Answer the questions in activity 8 according to the clues given.

I'm allergic.
No, I shouldn't.

a He is passionate about languages.
_____

b My allowance money is all gone.
_____

c Tickets are at a super sale discount.
_____

d The interest rates are very low now.
_____

e She is scared of blood.
_____

f It looks a bit yellow.
_____

DIGITAL LITERACY

Fact and Opinion

A Matter of Opinion

Panel 1: Dan, you spend too long in the shower! We must save water.

Panel 2: That's not what this expert says ... More than 70% of the world's water consumption is for agriculture. Families consume only 16%.

Panel 3: So there's no reason for you to save water at home ... It's a useless sacrifice.

Panel 4: Well, that's HIS OPINION! / Did you hear what he said? Agriculture is the biggest water user. We can't do anything about it!

Panel 5: Come on, Lil! A long, hot shower is so relaxing!

Panel 6: I think researchers should find ways to increase water-use efficiency in agriculture ... But I think we should also do our part and save water at home! / I strongly agree, Lily!

84 eighty-four

1 Read and listen. What do Daniel and Lily disagree about?

a The need to save water at home.
b The use of water in agriculture.

2 Read the comics again. Then underline the correct words.

a Daniel **usually** / **hardly ever** takes long showers.
b According to the man in the video, agriculture **is** / **isn't** the main consumer of water.
c According to the video's message, saving water at home **is** / **isn't** helpful.
d Lily **admits** / **doesn't admit** that families are not the biggest consumers of water.
e Lily and Grandma think **it's** / **it's not** worth saving water at home anyway.

3 Read about the difference between fact and opinion. Then write F for *fact* or O for *opinion*.

> A **fact** is a statement that can be confirmed by research or evidence. An **opinion** is someone's ideas or beliefs about a topic. It cannot be proven true or false.

a ☐ We must save water.
b ☐ More than 70% of the world's water consumption is for agriculture.
c ☐ Families use only 16% of the world's water consumption.
d ☐ Saving water at home is a useless sacrifice.
e ☐ A long, hot shower is so relaxing.
f ☐ I think researchers should find ways to increase water-use efficiency in agriculture.

4 Read the sentences in activity 3 again. Then match.

FACTS

OPINIONS

Language clues
- adjectives
- figures
- historical events
- "I think …"
- "In my opinion …"
- measurements
- *must* / *should*

5 Work in groups of 3-4. Do what is asked and then share your ideas with the class.

a Online content often combines facts and opinions. Does this occur in the video that Daniel was watching?
b Choose a piece of online content (text, video, post) that has caught your attention recently. Identify which parts of it are facts and which parts are opinions. Why is it important to know how to differentiate these parts?

GLOBAL CITIZENSHIP

Discussing Controversial Topics

- Are students allowed to use cell phones at your school?
- What do you think about the cell phone bans at some schools?
- Why is it important to understand different points of view on a controversial topic like this?

1 Two students are debating cell phone bans at schools on a podcast show. Read and listen to the information. Then answer the questions.

a Which student is against the ban? _____

b And which student is in favor of the ban? _____

Martin: Welcome to the Young Voices podcast! I'm Martin Smith and this is the podcast that gives young people a voice. Today we're going to discuss a controversial topic. Our school district recently announced that students will be banned from using cell phones in local schools. Today we invited two students who have different opinions on the topic. On one side we have 16-year-old Kevin Molina and on the other side 15-year-old Layla Anderson. Good evening, folks, and welcome to the show. I'll start with you, Layla. What is your opinion on the school district's decision? Do you agree that cell phones should be banned in schools?

Layla: Good evening, Martin. Yes, I agree with the decision. Cell phones are a constant distraction for us students. There are studies that prove this. One study published by the London School of Economics found that students in schools with phone bans got higher test scores. And get this: Low-performing students benefited the most.

Martin: And what do you think about it, Kevin? Do you agree that, without cell phones, students will focus on classes and learn better?

Kevin: Good evening, Martin. No, I disagree. There's no question that cell phones are distracting. But they can also be used for educational purposes. We young people live in a research-and-learn environment. When students want to know "Why leaves float on water," they are only a search away from the answer. Banning this powerful resource from schools is a step backwards. Classes will become boring. And, contrary to what is expected, student performance will fall.

Martin: Layla, what do you think of the problem raised by Kevin? ...

2 Read the podcast transcript again and answer.

a What is Layla's main argument?
_____
_____

Global Attitudes & Action

b What is Kevin's main argument?
_____
_____

c What evidence does Layla present to support her argument?
_____
_____
_____

d Kevin presents an example to support his argument. What is it?
_____
_____
_____

3 The arguments below could be used in this debate. Write L in the arguments that support Layla's point of view and K in the arguments that support Kevin's point of view.

a ☐ Students use cell phones for texting or entertainment instead of studying.

b ☐ Some students use cell phones to cheat. They store information on them to look at during a test or text friends about answers.

c ☐ Teachers can individualize learning by sending specific quizzes and content to each student's device.

d ☐ Students can record lessons and take voice notes to study at home later.

e ☐ Cell phones can be a tool for cyberbullying.

f ☐ Shy students who find it difficult to participate in class discussions can engage in online forums.

A Debate Podcast

Do you agree with Layla or Kevin? It's time to defend your viewpoints in a debate podcast.

DOING

1 Work in groups of four or five students. Choose the topic that will be discussed on your podcast show. You can continue the debate about banning cell phones at school or choose another topic. Here are some suggestions:
- Should children be allowed to use social media?
- Does social media help or hinder free speech?
- Teens shouldn't keep secrets from parents. Agree or disagree?
- Cyberbullying can be worse than real-life bullying. True or false?
- Specific video games can lead to violent behavior. True or false?

2 Divide the tasks within the group. Who will be the debaters? Who will be the podcast hosts?

3 Remember that for the show to be interesting, the debaters must defend different points of view.

4 If you are going to be one of the debaters, look for information and write your main arguments. Search for evidence to support your arguments, such as studies, examples, statistics.

5 If you're going to host the podcast, write a basic script. Plan how you will introduce the topic and the debaters as well as the main questions you will ask them.

RECORDING

1 Record the podcast using a cell phone. If possible, download a specific application for this.

2 During the recording, the podcast hosts must follow the script, and debaters must discuss the topic based on their notes.

3 Don't interrupt the other debater. Listen to his or her opinion with respect and attention.

4 Make references to the other debater's speech whenever possible. Show that you agree with him or her at least in part, as Kevin did when he said: "There's no question that cell phones are distracting."

5 Once the recording is finished, edit the podcast using the appropriate application and upload it to a folder shared with the class.

REFLECTING

1 Listen and comment on other groups' podcasts.

2 Discuss as a class:

a Did you find it easy or difficult to discuss controversial issues? Why?

b Did understanding different points of view on a controversial topic help you form your own opinion?

c What makes a debate productive and interesting?

IRREGULAR VERBS

Infinitive	Simple Past	Past Participle
be /bi/	was / were /wɑz/, /wɜr/	been /bin/, /bɪn/
begin /bɪˈgɪn/	began /bɪˈgæn/	begun /bɪˈgʌn/
break /breɪk/	broke /broʊk/	broken /ˈbroʊkən/
bring /brɪŋ/	brought /brɔt/	brought /brɔt/
build /bɪld/	built /bɪlt/	built /bɪlt/
buy /baɪ/	bought /bɔt/	bought /bɔt/
choose /tʃuz/	chose /tʃoʊz/	chosen /ˈtʃoʊz(ə)n/
come /kʌm/	came /keɪm/	come /kʌm/
do /du/	did /dɪd/	done /dʌn/
drink /drɪŋk/	drank /dræŋk/	drunk /drʌŋk/
drive /draɪv/	drove /droʊv/	driven /ˈdrɪv(ə)n/
eat /it/	ate /eɪt/	eaten /ˈit(ə)n/
fall /fɔl/	fell /fel/	fallen /ˈfɔlən/
find /faɪnd/	found /faʊnd/	found /faʊnd/
fly /flaɪ/	flew /flu/	flown /floʊn/
forget /fərˈget/	forgot /fərˈgɑt/	forgotten /fərˈgɑt(ə)n/
get /get/	got /gɑt/	got /gɑt/, gotten /ˈgɑt(ə)n/
give /gɪv/	gave /geɪv/	given /ˈgɪv(ə)n/
go /goʊ/	went /went/	gone /gɔn/
have /hæv/	had /həd/	had /həd/
hear /hɪr/	heard /hɜrd/	heard /hɜrd/
know /noʊ/	knew /nu/	known /noʊn/
learn /lɜrn/	learnt / learned /lɜrnt/, /ˈlɜrnəd/	learnt / learned /lɜrnt/, /ˈlɜrnəd/
leave /liv/	left /left/	left /left/
lose /luz/	lost /lɔst/	lost /lɔst/
make /meɪk/	made /meɪd/	made /meɪd/
meet /mit/	met /met/	met /met/
pay /peɪ/	paid /peɪd/	paid /peɪd/
put /pʊt/	put /pʊt/	put /pʊt/
read /rid/	read /red/	read /red/
run /rʌn/	ran /ræn/	run /rʌn/
say /seɪ/	said /sed/	said /sed/
see /si/	saw /sɔ/	seen /sin/
sell /sel/	sold /soʊld/	sold /soʊld/
sing /sɪŋ/	sang /sæŋ/	sung /sʌŋ/
sit /sɪt/	sat /sæt/	sat /sæt/
speak /spik/	spoke /spoʊk/	spoken /ˈspoʊkən/
take /teɪk/	took /tʊk/	taken /ˈteɪkən/
teach /titʃ/	taught /tɔt/	taught /tɔt/
tell /tel/	told /toʊld/	told /toʊld/
think /θɪŋk/	thought /θɔt/	thought /θɔt/
wear /wer/	wore /wɔr/	worn /wɔrn/
win /wɪn/	won /wʌn/	won /wʌn/
write /raɪt/	wrote /roʊt/	written /ˈrɪt(ə)n/

WORKBOOK

CONTENTS

Starter	**168**
Unit 1 – Technology	**170**
Vocabulary 1	Contemporary Technologies	170
Grammar 1	Review: Simple Past	171
Vocabulary 2	Jobs	173
Grammar 2	Review: Past Progressive	174
Grammar Check	175
Listening	175
Extension	176
Vocabulary Plus	Safety Equipment	177
Unit 2 – Unexpected but True	**178**
Vocabulary 1	Prepositions	178
Grammar 1	Review: Simple Past and Past Progressive; *when* and *while*	179
Vocabulary 2	*-ed* / *-ing* Adjectives	181
Grammar 2	Present and Past Tenses	182
Grammar Check	183
Listening	183
Extension	184
Vocabulary Plus	Natural Phenomena	185
Unit 3 – Celebrate!	**186**
Vocabulary 1	Clothes and Accessories	186
Grammar 1	*be going to*	187
Vocabulary 2	Weather and Seasons	189
Grammar 2	*must* / *must not*	190
Grammar Check	191
Listening	191
Extension	192
Vocabulary Plus	Closet Items	193
Unit 4 – Make a Difference	**194**
Vocabulary 1	Jobs	194
Grammar 1	*should* (Affirmative and Negative)	195
Vocabulary 2	Health Problems	197
Grammar 2	*should* (Questions and Short Answers)	198
Grammar Check	199
Listening	199
Extension	200
Vocabulary Plus	Places of Work	201

STARTER

Free-time Activities

1 Complete the sentences with the words in the box.

do (2×)   go to (2×)   play   read

a My parents _____ volunteer work at an urban wildlife rehabilitation center.

b I love to _____ video games with my younger cousins at my grandma's house.

c John and Mike _____ martial art and it really helps them to be more focused and relaxed.

d One of my favorite free-time activities is to _____ a book.

e My friends and I like to _____ the movies on Saturday evenings.

f We often meet our neighbors when we _____ the gym.

Character Adjectives and Formation of Adverbs

2 Complete with the opposite adjectives and write their adverb form.

dishonest   __honest__   __honestly__

a bad   _____   _____
b sad   _____   _____
c shy   _____   _____
d talkative   _____   _____

3 Complete the adverbs with the missing letters.

a ___ u i ___ ___ l ___
b c o r r ___ ___ ___ l y
c c ___ r ___ f ___ ___ l y
d ___ n g ___ ___ ___ y
e n ___ i ___ ___ ___ y
f s ___ ___ ___ ___ ___ ___ y

Rooms, Furniture, and Gadgets

4 Label the furniture and gadgets and the room where you usually find them.

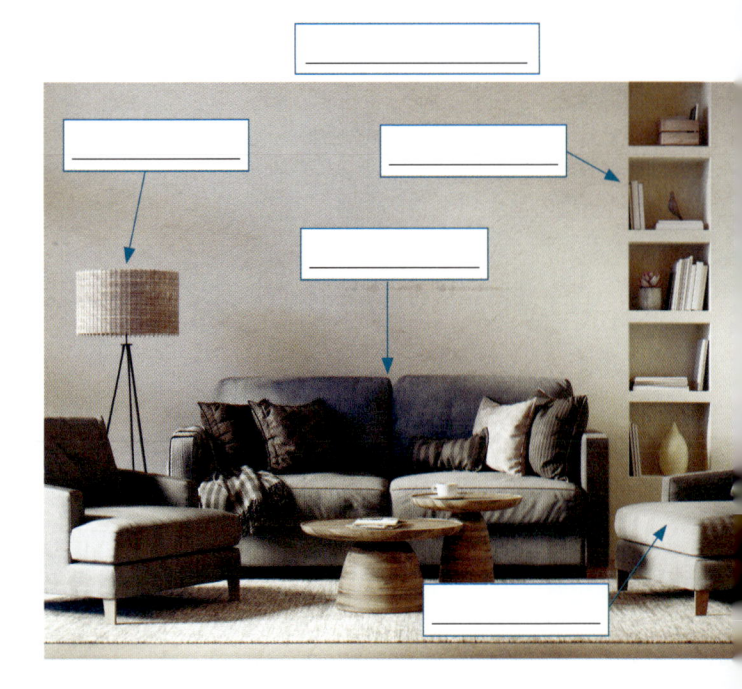

168 one hundred sixty-eight

STARTER

Places to Visit

5 Write the place each person should visit, according to their interests.

> cave   coastline   reef   ruin

a Maria wants to observe some undersea corals: _____

b Edward is fascinated by the remains of antique buildings: _____

c Lavaughn is really curious about underground formations: _____

d Jeremy likes sand, sea, and palm trees: _____

Comparatives and Superlatives

6 Look at the picture and complete the sentences with the comparative or the superlative form of the words in the box.

> long   old   short   tall   young

a Dean is _____ person in the family.
b Sarah's hair is _____ than Karen's.
c Frank is _____ than Lisa.
d Laura is Dean's and Sarah's _____ daughter.
e Sue is _____ than Larry.

Simple Present and Present Progressive

7 Complete the questions with the simple present or the present progressive form. Then find the answers in the box.

> I thought of something really funny.
> No, I'm studying.   On the weekends.
> To the library.   Yes, I do.

a Where _____ you _____ (go)?
_____

b When _____ you usually _____ (play) video games?
_____

c _____ you _____ (watch) TV now?
_____

d _____ you usually _____ (go) to school in the morning?
_____

e Why _____ you _____ (laugh)?
_____

Simple Past and Past Progressive

8 Write questions for the answers.

a _____
Last night I had dinner at 9pm.

b _____
When the teacher arrived, I was talking to my friend.

c _____
Yesterday I watched the new episode of *Greenhouse Academy* on TV.

d _____
The person I was talking to is my cousin Dan.

e _____
The most interesting book I read last year was *Around the World in Eighty Days*, by Jules Verne.

one hundred sixty-nine **169**

1 TECHNOLOGY

VOCABULARY 1

Contemporary Technologies

1 Order the letters and write the sentences.

a r a e t e c   a   y p s l l a i t   _create a playlist_

b h o s p   e l i n o n _____

c s u e   c i s o a l   k n e o w t r
   _____

d e u s   t i a e g r m s n   c e r v s e s i
   _____

e s e u   t u i r l a v   l a y e r i t
   _____

f s e u   i r i f t l i a a c   g n e n i t l c e l e i
   _____

2 Look at the pictures and match them with the technologies listed in activity 1.

3 Complete the sentences with the words in the box.

| e-book   metaverse   online   playlist   post |
| streaming   ~~upload~~   video   virtual |

I have some photos on my cell phone. How can I ___upload___ it onto the cloud storage service?

a There's an interesting story on my sister's social network. I want to _____ a comment.

b I'm working at home today, so the meeting will be by _____ conferencing.

c I love adventure movies, specially the ones with _____ reality.

d I don't want to lose this new series' episode. I will watch it on a _____ service.

e Can you create a music _____ on your cell phone?

f We don't have space at my bookcase. Let's buy an _____!

g Some schools are using _____ to simulate a hyperrealistic virtual environment to improve learning and make it easier and faster.

h I really need a new virtual reality headset, but it isn't available in my country. So I'm going to shop it _____.

UNIT 1

🔑 GRAMMAR 1

Review: Simple Past

1 Underline the correct options.

The movie **was** / **were** really boring.

a Where **was** / **were** you last night?

b Who **was** / **were** that girl at the video conferencing?

c Adam and Layla **wasn't** / **weren't** pleased about the comments on their social network.

d There **was** / **were** an amazing picture on that e-book.

e My cell phone **wasn't** / **weren't** a birthday present.

f **Was** / **Were** there a lot of free online games on that site?

2 Complete the sentences with *was* or *were*.

How old ___were___ you in 2013?

a Where _____ Andy's virtual reality headset?

b How _____ the video conferencing meeting yesterday?

c I _____ annoyed with her about the pictures of me on Facebook.

d There _____ a great online game about zombies at the shopping mall.

e What _____ Kate's video and music playlists like?

3 Correct the sentences. Write one negative and one affirmative sentence.

My favorite series were on my cell phone.
(✗ streaming service)
My favorite series weren't on my cell phone.
They were on a streaming service.

a My cell phone was under the bed. (✗ sofa)
_____
_____

b We were at the video conferencing yesterday afternoon. (✗ park)
_____
_____

c The Instagram post was from Adam. (✗ Alice)
_____
_____

d The games on that site were terrible. (✗ great)
_____
_____

4 Complete the text with the simple past form of the verbs in parentheses.

We ___visited___ (visit) the Computer History Museum in California last year. First, we **a** _____ (watch) a movie about the history of computers. They **b** _____ (show) us a strange computer from 1939 – the Atanasoff-Berry computer. It **c** _____ (look) like lots of light bulbs on a metal plate! In the movie there was also a huge calculator from 1940. They **d** _____ (call) it the Complex Number Calculator. George Stibitz **e** _____ (design) it. It **f** _____ (use) telephone wires to send the calculations to a machine in another city. After the movie, we **g** _____ (walk) around the museum with a guide. She **h** _____ (talk) about all the old computers.

5 Find the words in the word search to complete the sentences.

… of things   video …

play … games   … reality

augmented …   … intelligence

I	R	I	I	O	S	C	S	O	H	D	N
H	A	A	L	H	E	I	O	N	L	E	R
C	O	N	F	E	R	E	N	C	I	N	G
O	A	E	A	D	V	N	E	O	I	O	H
A	R	T	I	F	I	C	I	A	L	G	T
L	D	L	U	A	R	N	F	H	I	I	V
R	R	O	A	F	T	E	S	O	V	A	N
L	E	K	T	E	U	N	A	N	N	H	H
A	B	A	R	W	A	D	A	L	N	I	H
I	L	N	A	C	L	O	I	I	I	N	H
E	E	W	A	L	M	T	E	N	B	T	A
T	T	A	T	T	E	S	N	E	T	E	Y

6 Complete the text with the simple past form of the irregular verbs in parentheses.

I <u>had</u> (have) an amazing vacation last year. My grandmother **a** _____ (give) me some money and I **b** _____ (go) traveling with my friend Adam. Our vacation **c** _____ (begin) badly because Adam **d** _____ (lose) his passport in Paris. Luckily, the police **e** _____ (find) it for him. We **f** _____ (take) a train from Paris to the south of France. Then we **g** _____ (get) a boat to the island of Corsica. We **h** _____ (swim) every day, **i** _____ (eat) lots of delicious French food, and **j** _____ (make) friends with some Spanish people at the campground. Then we **k** _____ (fly) back to Austin.

7 Match the sentence beginnings with the endings. Then write the sentences in the simple past negative form.

a [3] I (not visit) you
b [ ] I (not call) you
c [ ] We (not watch) all of the movie
d [ ] I (not upload) his pictures
e [ ] We (not shop) the tickets online
f [ ] We (not buy) the e-book

1 because I (not have) my cell phone.
2 because we (not like) it.
3 because I (not have) your address.
4 because we (not know) the singer.
5 because he (not want) me to.
6 because we (not need) to.

a <u>I didn't visit you because I didn't have your address.</u>
b _____
c _____
d _____
e _____
f _____

8 Complete the questions and answers with the simple past form of the verbs in parentheses.

Ross Where <u>did you get</u> (you / get) your new cell phone?
Jane I **a** _____ (shop) it online.
Ross How much **b** _____ (it / cost)?
Jane I **c** _____ (pay) US$200 for it.

Pete **d** _____ (you / call) Ellie?
Carol No, I **e** _____ (send) her an email.
Pete What **f** _____ (you / say) in it?
Carol I **g** _____ (invite) her to a concert.

Sue When **h** _____ (Jo / break) her virtual reality headset?
Paul She **i** _____ (not break) it. She **j** _____ (leave) it at her cousin's house on Saturday.

Guy When **k** _____ (Tom / create) his playlist?
Jen He **l** _____ (do) it yesterday. It **m** _____ (not take) long.

9 Write a short answer and an extra sentence for each question.

Did you wake up early yesterday?
<u>Yes, I did.</u> (short answer)
<u>I woke up at 6:30.</u> (extra sentence)
<u>No, I didn't.</u> (short answer)
<u>I woke up at 10:30.</u> (extra sentence)

a Did you have breakfast this morning?
_____
_____

b Did your teacher give you homework yesterday?
_____
_____

c Did you post something on your Facebook profile yesterday?
_____
_____

d Did you leave your e-book at your friend's house?
_____
_____

UNIT 1

ABC VOCABULARY 2

Jobs

1 Match the jobs with the pictures.

- a [5] construction worker
- b [ ] researcher
- c [ ] teacher
- d [ ] doctor
- e [ ] firefighter
- f [ ] police officer
- g [ ] lawyer
- h [ ] artist

2 Match the word beginnings and endings to form job names.

- a journal   [ ] ian
- b politic   [ ] er
- c clean   [ ] ist
- d techni   [ ] cian

3 Read what some people say, guess the job, and write the answer.

Open your mouth, please. I need to check your throat.
doctor

a Someone dropped a cigarette and that's how the fire started. We managed to put it out and luckily nobody died.
_____

b The police say he did it. He says he didn't do it. I'm speaking for him in court.
_____

c I did these paintings ten years ago. It was my blue period and, as you can see, the main color in all of them is blue.
_____

d We're asking a million cell phone users to answer these questions. We want to find out: Are cell phones bad for us?
_____

e In our laboratory we're trying to make new kinds of sunscreen.
_____

f I'm arresting you on suspicion of robbery.
_____

g Today we are going to learn about technology.
_____

one hundred seventy-three **173**

GRAMMAR 2

Review: Past Progressive

1 Underline the correct options.

I **was** / were waiting for you outside.

a You was / **were** using the computer for a long time.

b She **was** / were writing a post when I arrived.

c We was / **were** shopping online.

d Josh and Lisa was / **were** creating video playlists this morning.

e It **was** / were raining early this morning when I woke up.

f You and Vicki was / **were** playing loud music last night.

2 Write sentences using the negative and affirmative forms of the past progressive.

Liam (✗ shop) online. He (✓ do) his history project.
Liam wasn't shopping online. He was doing his history project.

a I (✗ read) an e-book. I (✓ watch) a movie.
_____
_____

b He (✗ hang out) with his friends. He (✓ buy) a virtual reality headset.
_____
_____

c They (✓ use) streaming services. They (✗ do) their homework.
_____
_____

d We (✓ upload) pictures. We (✗ use) the scanner.
_____
_____

e You (✗ talk) on your cell phone. You (✓ play) an online game.
_____
_____

f She (✗ send) a message. She (✓ call) Josie.
_____
_____

3 Complete the questions and the answers with the past progressive form of the verbs in parentheses. Then match the questions with the answers.

a [2] Why _were you shouting_ (you / shout) at the dog?

b [ ] Who _____ (make) that noise last night?

c [ ] Where _____ (you / sit) in the concert?

d [ ] What _____ (your friends / do) on the computer?

e [ ] Why _____ (Rosie / stand) in the street with her cell phone?

1 I _____ (not sit).
I _____ (stand) at the back.

2 Because he _was eating_ (eat) my dinner.

3 She _____ (use) it to make a video.

4 Steve. He _____ (listen) to very loud rock music.

5 They _____ (check) their Facebook profiles.

4 Write questions using the past progressive form. Then write answers that are true for you.

What / you do / at five o'clock / on Saturday afternoon?
What were you doing at five o'clock on Saturday afternoon?
I was playing basketball in the park.

a What / you do / at ten o'clock / last night?
_____
_____
_____

b Where / you live / five years ago?
_____
_____
_____

c What / you wear / yesterday?
_____
_____
_____

d What / you think about / five minutes ago?
_____
_____
_____

e Who / you sit / next to / in the last math class?
_____
_____
_____

UNIT 1

GRAMMAR CHECK

1 Read the interview and circle the correct answers.

Julie Brinton tells Mark at #*InstaEnglish* about her experience with an online gym.

Mark Why **a** _____ you join it?

Julie I didn't **b** _____ time to go to the gym last summer. A friend told me about an online gym and I **c** _____ to try it. First, I **d** _____ questions about my height, weight, and age. Then a virtual trainer **e** _____ an exercise program for me.

Mark **f** _____ you get in shape?

Julie Yes, I **g** _____ . But there **h** _____ some problems.

Mark What kind of problems?

Julie When I **i** _____ exercises, it was often hard to see the screen. Then once, when I was lying on the floor, my cat **j** _____ on my face!

	1	2	3
a	have	(did)	do
b	had	has	have
c	was deciding	is deciding	decided
d	is answering	answered	was answering
e	chose	was choosing	choosed
f	Do	Were	Did
g	did	was	do
h	was	were being	were
i	was doing	did	am doing
j	jumped	jumps	was jumping

2 Listen and check your answers.

LISTENING

1 Listen to five teenagers talking about their ideal jobs. Match the letters a-e with the names.

Who …

a wants to be a scientist?
b wants to work in the music business?
c wants to work for justice in the world?
d wants to work with computers?
e wants to be a journalist?

1 ☐ Andrea
2 ☐ Joel
3 ☐ Tom
4 ☐ Mark
5 ☐ Rose

2 Listen again. Then write T for *true* or F for *false*.

a ☐ Andrea prefers TV to radio and newspapers.
b ☐ Joel is scared of blood.
c ☐ Mark can't act.
d ☐ Rose only wants to work in the USA.
e ☐ Tom is interested in spaceships.

EXTENSION

Circle the correct words to complete the text.

"What **a do / are** you want to be?" Why do people **b always ask / ask always** this question? My answer is always, "I **c didn't / don't** know." At age six, the answer **d were / was** easy for me – astronaut! Now, I **e like / liked** the idea of being a web designer. I'm **f always happy / happy always** to help friends with their technology issues. And I love **g do / doing** fun things with my computer. Yesterday, for example, I **h was / am** on the internet when I found some great design ideas. So I uploaded some old pictures at the cloud storage service. Then I **i drew / was drawing** some sketches on them with my digital pen and I **j was writing / wrote** words in a balloon coming out of someone's mouth. At the moment, I'm **k designing / design** a website for a friend. But my mom **l came / comes** into my room every ten minutes and **m says / said** helpful things like, "Why **n are you / you are** staying inside on a lovely day like today?" So things **o is / are** going very well!

UNIT 1

ABC VOCABULARY PLUS

Safety Equipment

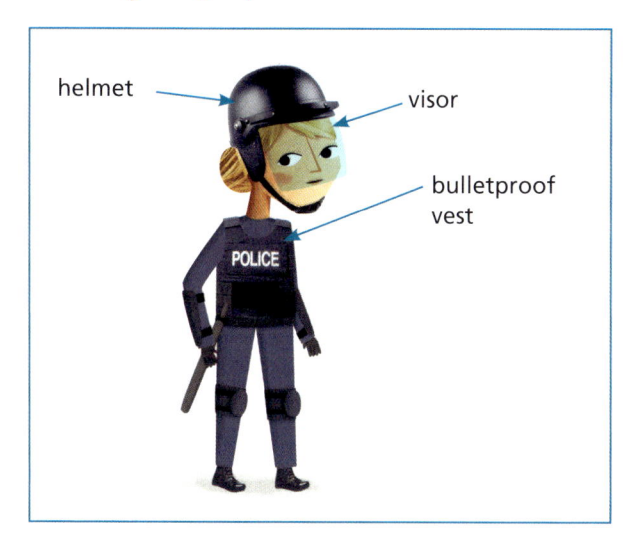

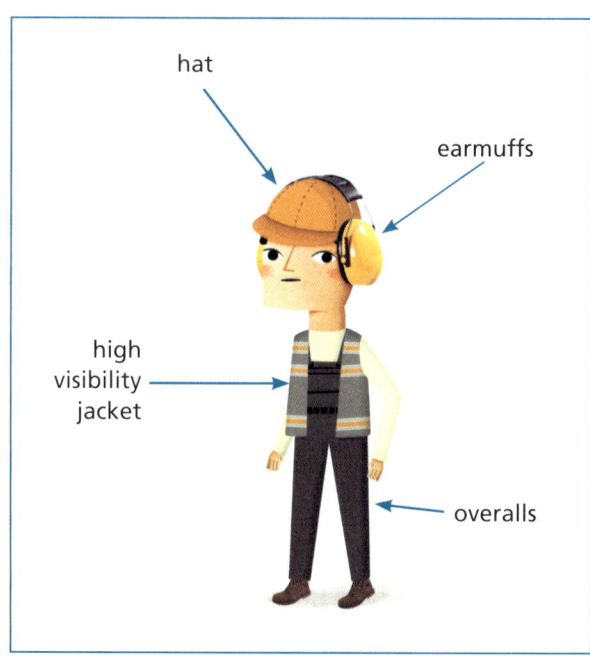

helmet
visor
bulletproof vest

safety glasses
face mask
disposable gloves

hat
earmuffs
high visibility jacket
overalls

1 Complete the chart with the words in the pictures. Then listen and check.

3))

head	eyes / face	ears	hands	body
hat				

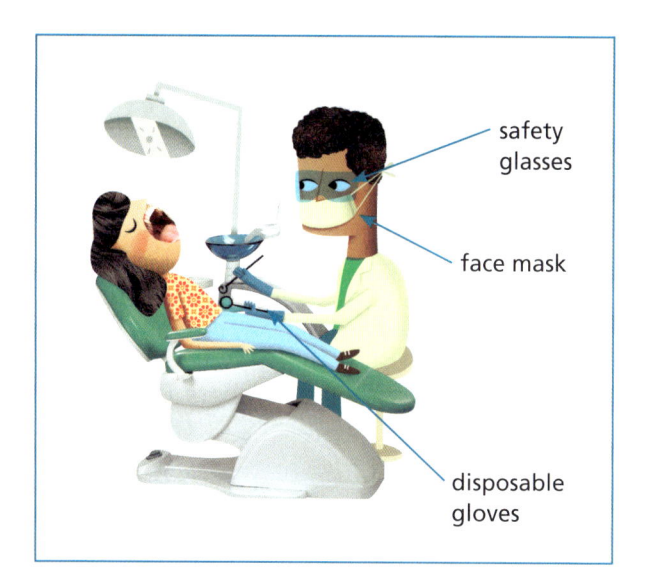

2 Underline the correct options.

An artist usually wears **overalls** / **a bulletproof vest**.

a A firefighter usually wears a **helmet** / **earmuffs**.

b A scientist often wears **a high visibility jacket** / **safety glasses**.

c A security guard usually wears a **bulletproof vest** / **face mask**.

d A doctor often wears **disposable gloves** / **a cap**.

e A construction worker often wears a **visor** / **high visibility jacket**.

3 Read the definitions and write the words.

These are made of rubber and they come in pairs.
disposable gloves

a This is made of fabric and it covers your mouth.
___

b This is always a bright color like yellow or orange.
___

c This is a head covering, but it isn't hard.
___

d This is made of plastic and it covers your face.
___

e These are made of plastic and they cover your eyes.
___

one hundred seventy-seven **177**

2

UNEXPECTED BUT TRUE

VOCABULARY 1

Prepositions

1 Match the words with numbers 1-12 in the pictures.

a [10] climb **out of**
b [ ] dive **into**
c [ ] climb **up**
d [ ] walk **along**
e [ ] sail **around**
f [ ] jump **over**
g [ ] run **toward**
h [ ] parachute **down**
i [ ] drive **away from**
j [ ] jump **through**
k [ ] swim **across**
l [ ] walk **under**

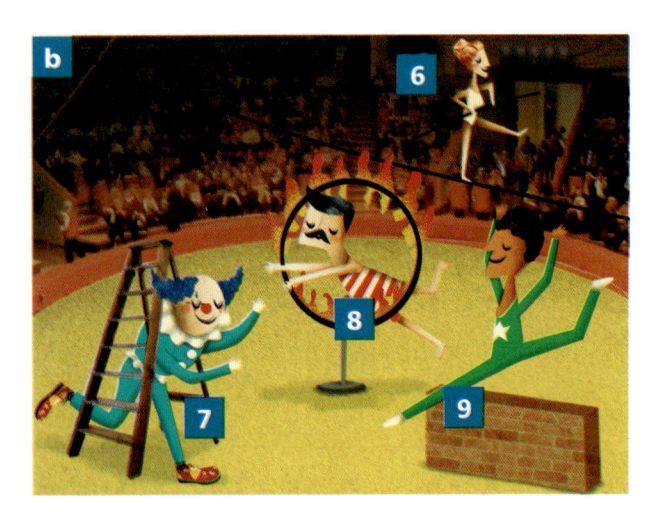

2 Complete the text with the prepositions in the box.

> across   along   ~~around~~   away from   down   into   out of   over   under   up

I had a strange dream last night. I was looking at a beautiful lake with an island in the middle. A boat was sailing __around__ the island. I felt hot, so I dove **a** _____ the lake and started swimming **b** _____ it. When I got to the other side, I climbed **c** _____ the lake and lay in the sun. Then a plane flew **d** _____ me and a man parachuted **e** _____ to the grass. It was Simon. I waved at him, but he got into a car and drove **f** _____ the lake. Then I saw a river. There was a path next to the river and a bridge over it. I started walking **g** _____ the path. I walked **h** _____ the bridge and found a mountain in front of me. My best friend was at the top of the mountain, so I wanted to run **i** _____ it, but suddenly I couldn't move. That's when I woke up.

UNIT 2

🔑 GRAMMAR 1

Review: Simple Past and Past Progressive; *when* and *while*

1 Circle the correct words.

We were sleeping on the beach **while** / **when** somebody stole our camera.

a **While** / **When** they were cooking sausages on the beach, it started to rain.

b Where were you going **while** / **when** we met you?

c Were you watching the game **while** / **when** I called you?

d **While** / **When** I wasn't watching, she jumped out of the tree.

e We were cycling in the forest **while** / **when** we saw the bear.

2 Complete the sentences with the past progressive form of the verbs in parentheses.

I _____was diving_____ (dive) into the lake when I hit my head.

a She fell over while she _____ (run) to catch the bus.

b Who _____ (you / talk) to when I saw you this morning?

c He lost his keys while he _____ (climb) over the wall.

d _____ (she / play) soccer when she hurt her leg?

e What _____ (you / do) while he _____ (make) dinner?

f _____ (they / sit) in their living room when the thief broke the window?

3 Circle the correct options.

I **fixed** / **was fixing** my bike when Fred **sent** / **was sending** me a text.

a She **found** / **was finding** the letter from Alex while she **cleaned** / **was cleaning** her room.

b They **played** / **were playing** soccer when she **broke** / **was breaking** her leg.

c He **fell** / **was falling** out of the tree while he **picked** / **was picking** fruit.

d He **did** / **was doing** the dishes when he **cut** / **was cutting** his finger on a knife.

e While we **watched** / **were watching** TV, somebody **knocked** / **was knocking** on the door.

4 Order the words to make sentences.

living / Martin / met / were / when / Where / you / you ?
Where were you living when you met Martin?

a A bird / my breakfast / flew / having / I / into / the kitchen / was / while
_____
_____

b at / her bag / bus stop / a man / She / standing / stole / the / was / when
_____
_____

c engine trouble / flying / over / the sea / started / the / The plane / was / when
_____
_____

d saw / shark / swimming / the / the island / to / We / we / were / when
_____
_____

e getting / I / I / into / saw / snake / my tent / a / was / While
_____
_____

f the beach / they / some treasure / were / found / While / along / walking / they
_____
_____

one hundred seventy-nine **179**

5 Complete the sentences with the simple past or the past progressive form of the verbs in parentheses.

It _____started_____ (start) to rain while we _____were having_____ (have) a picnic.

a I _____ (not answer) the phone because I _____ (have) my dinner.

b _____ (you / see) anything strange while you _____ (walk) by the river?

c I _____ (woke) you up because you _____ (talk) in your sleep.

d What _____ (Katrin / wear) when you _____ (see) her yesterday?

e She _____ (not hear) the bell because she _____ (listen) to very loud music.

f While she _____ (write) an email, the computer _____ (stop) working.

6 Write sentences using the past progressive or the simple past form of the verbs.

While / I get / a glass of water / the cat / eat / my lunch
While I was getting a glass of water, the cat ate my lunch.

a My pet hamster / hide / in my suitcase / while / I pack / it
_____
_____
_____

b He crash / into another car / because / he talk / on his cell phone
_____
_____
_____

c Who drive / when / they have / the accident?
_____
_____

d Where you sit / when / you see / the spaceship?
_____
_____

e We dance / at a party / when / we hear / a terrible crash
_____
_____
_____

7 Complete the text with the past progressive or the simple past form of the verbs in parentheses.

Andrew Philips _____was surfing_____ (surf) with a friend in California when a shark **a** _____ (attack) him. "I **b** _____ (lie) on my surfboard, because I was tired, when suddenly a huge black shape **c** _____ (appear) in the water," Andrew said. Andrew **d** _____ (shout) to his friend, Tom, but Tom **e** _____ (not understand). So Andrew **f** _____ (start) to swim very fast. "I **g** _____ (try) not to think about the danger while I **h** _____ (swim)," he told newspaper reporters. The shark **i** _____ (bite) Andrew's arm twice. "It **j** _____ (not hurt) very much, but there was a lot of blood and I was very frightened. Then, suddenly, six or seven dolphins **k** _____ (swim) toward me. They **l** _____ (make) a circle around me and **m** _____ (stop) the shark from getting near me. While I **n** _____ (swim) toward the shore, the dolphins **o** _____ (keep) me safe." Andrew **p** _____ (get) very weak and tired when, luckily, Neil Turner, of the coast guard, **q** _____ (see) him.

"I **r** _____ (get) into my boat immediately and **s** _____ (go) to help him," Neil said. "The water around Andrew was very red because he **t** _____ (still lose) a lot of blood. I **u** _____ (lift) him out of the water immediately and **v** _____ (take) him back to the shore. When the boat **w** _____ (arrive) at the shore, a medical team **x** _____ (already wait) for Andrew. They **y** _____ (give) him first aid and **z** _____ (drive) him to the hospital."

UNIT 2

ABC VOCABULARY 2

-ed / -ing Adjectives

1 Look at the pictures and complete the words.

a bor_____
b bor___ing___
c annoy_____
d annoy_____
e excit_____  
f excit_____
g tir_____
h frighten_____ 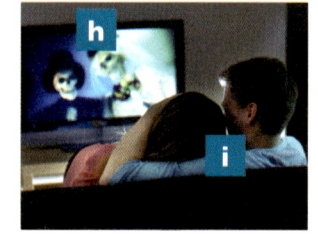 
i frighten_____
j tir_____
k worr_____  
l worr_____
m interest_____
n surprise_____  
o surpris_____
p interest_____

2 Circle the correct words.

She borrows my things and doesn't give them back. It's very **annoyed** / (**annoying**).

a He travels a lot and tells great stories. He's a very **interested** / **interesting** person.
b We're going on vacation tomorrow. I'm really **excited** / **exciting**.
c I'm very **worried** / **worrying** because I can't find my passport anywhere.
d I didn't expect to get a good grade. I was very **surprised** / **surprising**.
e The waves were really big and I'm not a good swimmer. It was **frightened** / **frightening**.

3 Complete the sentences with the words in the box.

| annoyed   bored   boring   exciting |
| frightened   frightening   ~~interested~~ |
| tired   tiring |

Are you ___interested___ in birds? There's a big green one in that tree.

a Let's take the elevator to the seventh floor. Walking up the stairs is too _____.
b I got _____ with my brother last night. He was making a lot of noise and I couldn't sleep.
c I don't watch horror movies. They're too _____ for me.
d I was _____ in that class, so I started to think about the holidays.
e I'm _____ because I didn't sleep last night. I must go to bed early tonight.
f This book is very _____. I can't stop reading it.
g The bull started to run at me and I was really _____.
h The movie was really _____. I fell asleep in the middle of it.

4 Complete the sentences so they are true for you.

a I am frightened of _____.
b I think _____ is boring.
c When I'm annoyed, I _____.
d I was surprised when _____.
e I'm interested in _____.

one hundred eighty-one **181**

GRAMMAR 2

Present and Past Tenses

1 What tenses are the underlined verbs? Write *simple present*, *present progressive*, *simple past*, or *past progressive*.

Emma Why <u>are you wearing</u> that silly hat?
present progressive

Noah I always <u>wear</u> a hat in the sun.
simple present

Emma **a** <u>Did you get</u> it in Florida?
_____

Noah **b** Yes, I <u>bought</u> it at a market.
_____

Emma **c** What <u>were you doing</u> in Florida?
_____

Noah **d** My parents <u>took</u> me there for vacation.
_____

Emma **e** <u>Do you go</u> there every year?
_____

Noah **f** No. We <u>went</u> there last year because my uncle <u>was living</u> there.
_____

Emma **g** Where's <u>he living</u> now?
_____

Noah **h** Scotland. I <u>want</u> to go there for New Year.
_____

2 Match the sentences. Then complete with the correct form of the verbs in parentheses.

a ☐ 3 While I ___wasn't looking___ (not look),
b ☐   What _____ (you / do)
c ☐   She _____ (drop) all the plates
d ☐   He always _____ (wear) a suit and tie
e ☐   Look at them! They _____ (smile)
f ☐   I _____ (crash) the car last year
g ☐   Josie _____ (not speak) today

1 because I was driving too fast.
2 because someone is taking their picture.
3 my little sister hid my keys under my bed.
4 when he goes to work.
5 because she has a sore throat.
6 when she heard the terrible news.
7 when you found the scorpion in your tent?

3 Complete the text with the correct form of the verbs in parentheses. Use the simple present, the present progressive, the simple past, or the past progressive.

Last summer, I __was staying__ (stay) in my little house by the sea when something very strange **a** _____ (happen). I **b** _____ (watch) the sunset when, suddenly, a boy of about 10 **c** _____ (appear) from nowhere. He **d** _____ (hold) a big white towel and his hair was wet. I **e** _____ (notice) a chain around his neck with the letter "C" on it. He said, "My sister, Gaby, swam out to Burnt Island. Now she **f** _____ (try) to swim back, but the current is very strong. She **g** _____ (drown). Please do something." I **h** _____ (go) to my boat, but the boy **i** _____ (not come) with me. Suddenly, he wasn't there. I **j** _____ (take) the boat toward Burnt Island and **k** _____ (find) Gaby. She **l** _____ (not swim) and she **m** _____ (lie) with her face in the water. I **n** _____ (pull) her into the boat. She was very weak, but she was alive. "Thank you," she said, "I **o** _____ (drown). You **p** _____ (save) my life." "Your brother did," I **q** _____ (answer). "He **r** _____ (tell) me to help you." Gaby **s** _____ (start) to cry. "I don't have a brother," she said. "Charlie **t** _____ (drown) near Burnt Island last year. He was only 10 years old. I **u** _____ (think) about him every day. This was his chain. I always **v** _____ (wear) it now." She **w** _____ (show) me the chain around her neck. It was the same chain as the boy's.

UNIT 2

GRAMMAR CHECK

1 Read the text and circle the correct answers.

You probably know about hypnotists. They **a** _____ into a person's eyes and that person **b** _____ to sleep. Tanya Brooks, a talented hypnotist, and her friend **c** _____ a picnic in Yellowstone National Park when a dangerous bear came up to them. They were both so frightened, they **d** _____ away. But then, Tanya **e** _____ an excellent idea. She **f** _____ up and looked into the eyes of the bear. While she was doing this, it suddenly **g** _____ asleep. Then, Tanya and her friend **h** _____ into their car and drove away. Now, she **i** _____ a book about hypnotizing dangerous animals. But be careful! It usually **j** _____.

	1	2	3
a	are looking	(look)	were looking
b	went	is going	goes
c	are having	had	were having
d	aren't running	didn't run	weren't running
e	was having	has	had
f	stood	was standing	stands
g	is falling	fell	was falling
h	were getting	did get	got
i	writes	is write	is writing
j	doesn't work	wasn't working	isn't working

2 Listen and check your answers.

LISTENING

1 Listen and number the events in the correct order.

- a ☐ Joss got her sweater from her bedroom.
- b ☐ Joss met a girl on the stairs.
- c ☐ Joss saw a light in her bedroom window.
- d ☐ Joss took a picture of a girl in her window.
- e ☐ Joss took some pictures of the lake.
- f ☐ Joss walked around the garden.
- g ☐ Joss went to stay with Leonie.
- h ☐ Joss looked for her picture of Betsy.
- i ☐ Leonie started practicing the piano.
- j ☐ Leonie told Joss about Betsy.

2 Listen again and write T for *true*, F for *false*, or DK for *don't know*.

- a There were usually a lot of visitors at Leonie's house. ☐
- b Joss doesn't have any brothers or sisters. ☐
- c Joss didn't know the girl on the stairs. ☐
- d Joss was not surprised to see the light in her room. ☐
- e The girl with the pink flower was trying to use Joss's camera. ☐
- f Betsy was one of Leonie's cousins. ☐
- g Joss's picture did not show Betsy. ☐

EXTENSION

Underline the correct options to complete the text.

Last weekend, I **a was staying / stayed** at Gary's house in the country. Gary and I **b was / were** lying in the sun in the garden. I was trying to read a difficult philosophy book, but Gary's dog was making noise, so I **c didn't / don't** understand anything. Gary's dog loves **d to chase / chasing** after his ball, so I **e threw / was throwing** it for him. I was surprised because he **f didn't / wasn't** come back to me with it. After a bit, I **g was going / went** to look for him. He **h was / is** under a tree with a very long white bone. I got Gary to look at it. He **i studies / is studying** medicine now, so he knows about bones. Gary **j said / was saying** it's definitely a human bone. My question is: Where **k did / does** the dog find it? And how and when did that person **l die / died**?

UNIT 2

VOCABULARY PLUS

Natural Phenomena

1 _____ 2 _____ 3 _____ 4 _____ 5 _____

6 _____ 7 _____ 8 _____ 9 _____ 10 _____

1 Label the pictures with the words in the box. Then listen and repeat.

🔊 6

> avalanche   blizzard   cyclone   drought
> hailstorm   heat wave   landslide
> thunderstorm   tsunami   wildfire

2 Underline the correct words.

There is often **a drought** / **an avalanche** in hot countries in the summer.

a It was snowing and then it became a **blizzard** / **landslide**.

b The **tsunami** / **wildfire** started in the forest.

c The **drought** / **cyclone** destroyed everything in its path.

d The dark clouds were followed by a **hailstorm** / **wildfire**.

e **Thunderstorms** / **Blizzards** often occur in very hot weather.

3 Complete the definitions with the correct words.

A ___tsunami___ is an enormous wave in the sea.

a An _____ is when a lot of snow moves down a mountain.

b A _____ is an extremely strong rotating wind.

c A _____ is when it is unusually hot for several days or weeks.

d A _____ is when there isn't any rain for months.

e A _____ is when a lot of earth moves down a mountain.

4 Complete these sentences so they are true for you. Try to use words from activity 1.

a In my country, there are sometimes _____.

b I have never seen _____.

c I am scared of _____.

one hundred eighty-five **185**

3
CELEBRATE!

VOCABULARY 1

Clothes and Accessories

1 Order the letters and write the words. Then match them with the pictures.

- [4] h t s r i -T — T-shirt
- [ ] k j e t a c — _____
- [ ] s i r k t — _____
- [ ] r k s n e s a e — _____
- [ ] r s f a c — _____
- [ ] n j s a e — _____
- [ ] t s o b o — _____
- [ ] t s r i h — _____
- [ ] r s d e s — _____
- [ ] t w s e r e a — _____
- [ ] o t a c — _____
- [ ] s t n p a — _____
- [ ] t s s r h o — _____

2 Where do the clothes go? Write the words from activity 1 in the correct group.

- **a** on your neck _____
- **b** on your body _____
- **c** on your legs _____
- **d** on your feet _____

3 Read the clues and complete the crossword.

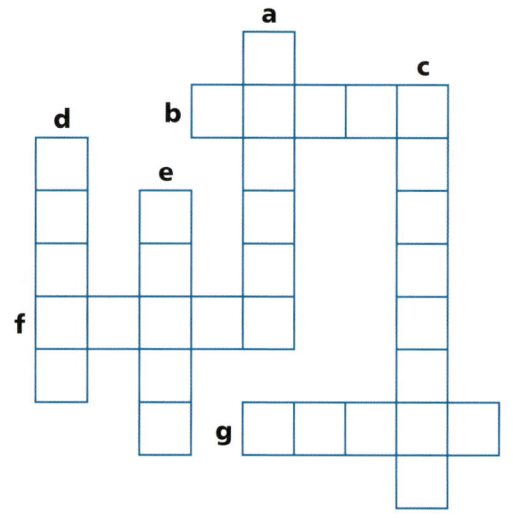

Down
- **a** A light coat.
- **c** You wear a pair of these on your feet when you're doing exercise.
- **d** It's only one piece and it covers your body.
- **e** You wear this on the top of your body. It's light and has buttons on the front.

Across
- **b** Jeans are an example of a pair of these.
- **f** Men don't usually wear this.
- **g** You wear this on your neck to keep warm.

4 Complete the sentences so that is true for you.

- **a** Today I'm wearing _____.
- **b** Yesterday I wore _____.
- **c** On weekends I usually wear _____.

UNIT 3

🔑 GRAMMAR 1

be going to

1 Underline the correct words.

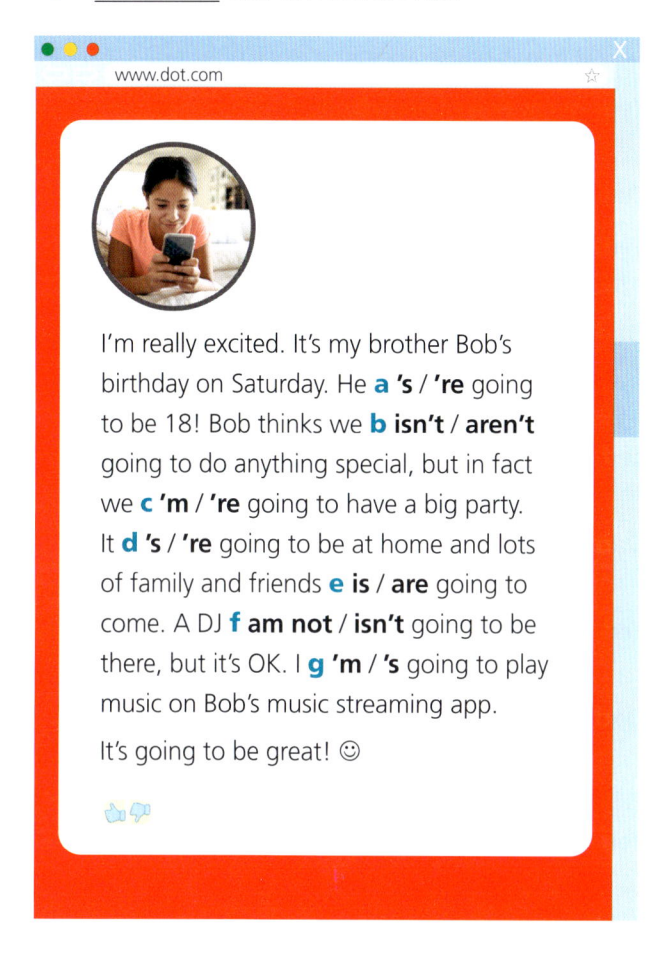

---
www.dot.com

I'm really excited. It's my brother Bob's birthday on Saturday. He **a 's / 're** going to be 18! Bob thinks we **b isn't / aren't** going to do anything special, but in fact we **c 'm / 're** going to have a big party. It **d 's / 're** going to be at home and lots of family and friends **e is / are** going to come. A DJ **f am not / isn't** going to be there, but it's OK. I **g 'm / 's** going to play music on Bob's music streaming app. It's going to be great! 😊

👍 👎

---

2 Rewrite the sentences using the information in parentheses.

Bob's going to be unhappy on Saturday night. (happy)
Bob isn't going to be unhappy on Saturday night.
He's going to be happy.

a One thousand people are going to come to the party. (one hundred)
_____
_____

b Bob's going to receive two presents. (lots of)
_____
_____

c I'm going to wear a dress. (pants)
_____
_____

d The party's going to finish at ten o'clock. (eleven o'clock)
_____
_____

3 Complete the text with the *going to* form of the verbs in parentheses.

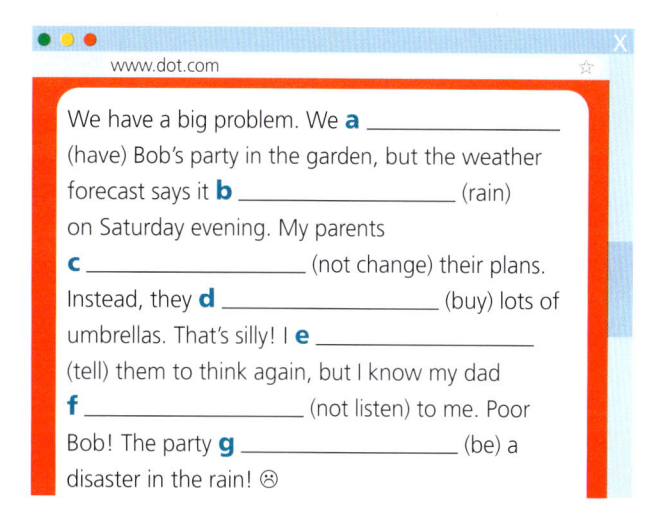

---
www.dot.com

We have a big problem. We **a** _____ (have) Bob's party in the garden, but the weather forecast says it **b** _____ (rain) on Saturday evening. My parents **c** _____ (not change) their plans. Instead, they **d** _____ (buy) lots of umbrellas. That's silly! I **e** _____ (tell) them to think again, but I know my dad **f** _____ (not listen) to me. Poor Bob! The party **g** _____ (be) a disaster in the rain! ☹

---

4 Look at Mark's diary and write sentences with the affirmative or negative form of *going to*.

⭐ MONDAY ← (today)   get up early – do judo 7pm
⭐ TUESDAY   no school! go to the movies
⭐ WEDNESDAY   meet Sarah – play basketball 😊
⭐ THURSDAY   buy new jeans
⭐ FRIDAY   go swimming with Leo
⭐ SATURDAY
⭐ SUNDAY   visit grandparents

a Mark / get up early / today
_____

b he / do judo / tonight
_____

c he / go to school / on Tuesday
_____

d Mark and Sarah / play basketball / on Wednesday
_____

e Mark / buy new sneakers / on Thursday
_____

f Mark and Leo / go surfing / on Friday
_____

g he / visit grandparents / on the weekend
_____

5 Write sentences about your future plans.

a Tonight _____.
b Next Thursday _____.
c On the weekend _____.

6 Complete the questions with *is* or *are*. Then match and write the answers in the box with the correct questions.

> No, he isn't.   No, we aren't.
> Some soccer shoes.
> ~~Yes, I am.~~   Yes, it is.   Yes, they are.

__Are__ you going to go shopping this Saturday?
Yes, I am.

a What ___ you going to look for?
_____

b _____ your dad going to drive you to the mall?
_____

c _____ you and Ed going to play soccer next Sunday?
_____

d _____ your parents going to buy the shoes?
_____

e _____ it going to be an expensive day for them?
_____

7 Order the words to make questions. Then write short answers.

going / Gemma / sunbathe / Is / to ? (✓)
Is Gemma going to sunbathe?
Yes, she is.

a swim / Are / to / going / they ? (✓)
_____
_____

b to / play / they / going / Are / tennis ? (✗)
_____
_____

c Is / rain / to / going / it ? (✓)
_____
_____

d cook / she / to / Is / going ? (✗)
_____
_____

e your dad / go / going / Is / skiing / to ? (✓)
_____
_____

f a coat / she / going / Is / to / wear ? (✗)
_____
_____

8 Complete the questions with the correct *going to* form of the verbs in parentheses. Complete the short answers.

Ted What **a** _____ (you / do) this Saturday night, dad?

Dad Your mom and I are going to go to a party at Emma's house at eight o'clock.

Ted What type of party **b** _____ (it / be)?

Dad A costume party.

Ted Really? **c** _____ (you / buy) a costume?

Dad No, **d** _____. I'm going to make a cowboy costume. I'm going to wear a red shirt, boots and a big hat.

Ted A cowboy! **e** _____ (mom / go) as a cowgirl?

Dad Yes, **f** _____. She will wear boots too.

Ted **g** _____ (all the men / go) in costumes?

Dad Yes, **h** _____.
i _____ (you / see) your friends on Saturday night, Ted?

Ted Yes, **j** _____, but not before eight.

Dad Why not?

Ted Because I want to take some pictures of you – as a cowboy!

9 Answer the questions for you. Write full sentences.

a What are you going to do this weekend?
_____

b Where are you going to go?
_____

c Who are you going to see?
_____

d What are you going to wear?
_____

UNIT 3

ABC VOCABULARY 2

Weather and Seasons

1 Write the words in the box under the correct picture.

> cloudy   cold   dry   hot   mild   rainy
> snowy   stormy   sunny   warm   ~~wet~~   windy

wet

a _____
b _____
c _____
d _____
e _____
f _____
g _____
h _____
i _____
j _____
k _____

2 Complete the sentences with the seasons in the northern hemisphere.

March, April, and May are in _spring_.

a December, January, and February are in _____.

b September, October, and November are in _____.

c June, July, and August are in _____.

3 Look at the pictures and write sentences about the weather in the countries.

In Australia _____it's hot and dry_____.

a In France _____.

b In Brazil _____.

c In Canada _____.

d In China _____.

one hundred eighty-nine **189**

🔑 GRAMMAR 2

must / must not

1 Complete the rules with *must* or *must not*.

POOL RULES

a You __must__ wear a swimming cap.

You _____ eat or drink.

b People _____ run.

c You _____ swim in the correct lane.

d You _____ listen to the lifeguard.

e Swimmers _____ play ball games.

2 Rewrite the sentences using the pronouns in parentheses and *must* or *must not*.

Sit next to the window. (She)
She must sit next to the window.

a Don't eat in class. (You)
_____

b Don't touch the video projector. (They)
_____

c Listen to the teacher. (We)
_____

d Do the homework again. (He)
_____

e Don't wear these sneakers at school. (I)
_____

3 Look at the pictures and match the beginnings a-f to the endings 1-6. Then write sentences with the phrases *You must* or *You must not*.

a	[2] take pictures	1	on the plane
b	☐ drive on the left	2	in the museum
c	☐ talk on the phone	3	in the movie theater
d	☐ give any food	4	into the store
e	☐ take dogs	5	in Australia
f	☐ wear a seatbelt	6	to the animals

You must not take pictures in the museum.

UNIT 3

GRAMMAR CHECK

1 Read the dialogue and circle the correct answers.

Tina Hi, mom.
Mom Hi, Tina. What time **a** ___ going to be home?
Tina I'm just trying on a T-shirt and then I **b** ___ to come home.
Mom A T-shirt? Are you going **c** ___ it?
Tina Yes, **d** ___. It's really cool.
Mom What color **e** ___ to get?
Tina Black.
Mom Black? **f** ___ a black one, Tina. That **g** ___ going to be good for summer. How about a yellow one?
Tina No, mom. I **h** ___ going to buy a yellow T-shirt. I hate yellow! Look! I **i** ___ pay for the T-shirt so I can leave the store and go home. I have to go now. Bye!
Mom Tina? Wait a minute! Tina!

	1	2	3
a	you	you are	(are you)
b	'm going	'm go	going
c	buy	to buy	buys
d	am	I do	I am
e	are you going	are going you	you are going
f	Get	Don't get	Doesn't get
g	no	is aren't	isn't
h	isn't	'm not	aren't
i	must not	have not	must

2 Listen and check your answers.

7))

LISTENING

1 Listen to the dialogue and check (✓) the picture of Phoebe. Which city is she going to visit next month?

8))

_____

☐

☐

2 Listen again and answer the questions.

8))

a Who is Phoebe going to go away with?
_____
b When did she go to Vancouver?
_____
c Why didn't she go skiing there?
_____
d What's the weather like in Aspen today?
_____
e Where does Phoebe look at the weather forecast?
_____
f Which clothes does Matt think she's going to need?
_____

EXTENSION

Underline the correct options to complete the text.

a You love / **Do you love** skiing and also going to pop concerts? If the answer is *yes*, then you should go to Méribel in March next year. Why? Because **b** is / **there's** a music festival there called *Little World Festival*. For five days **c** they / **you** can ski or snowboard during the day and then listen to some of the top DJs and pop bands at night. Méribel is a beautiful ski resort in the French Alps. **d** Ago a few years / **A few years ago**, the band *The Feeling* went skiing there. During their vacation, they **e** **played** / 're playing a free concert outdoors on the piste for around 6,000 people. Everyone **f** was loving / **loved** it, so the band decided to create a new annual music festival. The first *Little World Festival* **g** **was** / were in March 2010. I **h** learn / **'m learning** to ski right now. I **i** don't go / **'m not** skiing outdoors because it doesn't often snow where I live in the USA. I can ski **j** **fast** / fastly now! I think *Little World Festival* sounds great! I **k** **'m going to go** / go there next year with some friends.

UNIT 3

VOCABULARY PLUS

Closet Items

1 Translate these words into your language. Then listen and repeat.

earrings	flip-flops
gloves	rain boots
sandals	slippers
sun hat	tie
umbrella	waterproof jacket

2 Label the picture with the words from activity 1.

3 Do you wear these accessories on your feet (F), hands (H), or body (B)?

- [F] flip-flops
- a ☐ gloves
- b ☐ sandals
- c ☐ tie
- d ☐ waterproof jacket
- e ☐ rain boots

4 Complete the sentences with words from activity 1.

When you come into the house, take off your shoes and put on your ____slippers____.

a It's rainy, put on your _____ and a _____. Don't forget your _____.

b We're going to the beach. Bring your _____ for your head and wear _____ on your feet.

c In many schools, you can't wear very long _____ in your ears.

d At weddings, the groom wears a _____ and the bride sometimes wears white _____.

5 Complete the sentences so that is true for you. Try to use words from activity 1.

a If I go to a birthday party, I'll wear _____.

b In winter, I usually wear _____.

c If it is raining, I always put on my _____.

one hundred ninety-three **193**

4 MAKE A DIFFERENCE

ABC VOCABULARY 1

Jobs

1 Look at the pictures and complete the crossword.

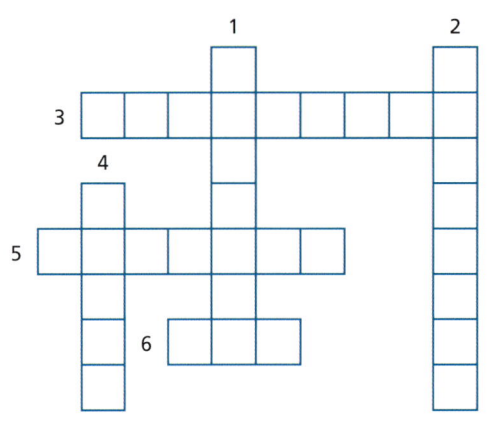

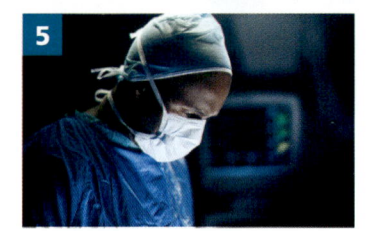

2 Match the words in the box with the places where the people work.

> actor   conservation scientist
> nurse   psychologist   surgeon   ~~teacher~~

   in a school   _teacher_

   a in an environmental department   _____

   b at the theater   _____

   c at the operating room   _____

   d in a hospital   _____

   e in a mental health center   _____

3 Complete with the corresponding words.

   a I'm looking for an interesting job that deals with animals. I love them! I want to be a _____.

   b I'm interested in science and how our bodies work. I can work very hard. I could be a _____.

   c I am interested in how communication gives access to people. I'm going to be a _____.

   d I like swimming, and I'm really good at it. I want to travel and be rich! I want to be an _____.

   e I'm interested in social issues, I want a job which I can help others with. I'm going to be a _____.

UNIT 4

🔑 GRAMMAR 1

should (Affirmative and Negative)

1 Underline the correct words.

You **should** / shouldn't sleep more than five hours every night.

a Your friends **should** / **shouldn't** remember your birthday!
b You **should** / **shouldn't** eat a lot of ice cream and cake.
c You **should** / **shouldn't** drink a lot of water.
d Vets **should** / **shouldn't** like animals.
e You **should** / **shouldn't** go swimming after eating.
f Drivers **should** / **shouldn't** text while driving.
g Students **should** / **shouldn't** relax in their free time.

2 Complete the sentences with *should* or *shouldn't* and the verbs in parentheses.

She ____should work____ harder at school – she wants to be an engineer. (work)

a You _____ chocolate now, it's too late. (eat)
b He _____ his teeth more often – they're dirty! (clean)
c We _____ his laptop without permission. (borrow)
d You _____ a fire outside in summer – it's dangerous. (build)
e Young children _____ coffee. (drink)
f I _____ my homework now before it's too late. (do)
g They _____ in the rain (run).

3 Use the clues and *should* or *shouldn't* to create green tips.

food waste / increase
We shouldn't increase food waste.

a use / leftovers / to cook / also
_____

b throw away / clothes / condition / old / good / in
_____

c donate / old / repair / clothes / or
_____

d the / bags / supermarket / buy / plastic / at
_____

e our / the / bring / own / to / bags / supermarket
_____

f drive / vehicles / private
_____

g transportation / instead / take / public
_____

4 Match the problems and recommendations to write advice sentences with *should* or *shouldn't*.

a I can't get to sleep after a long time in bed.
b I do lots of exercise and don't lose weight.
c I get too nervous before tests.
d I waste all my money on computer games.
e I'm having trouble making friends at my new school.

☐ join a book club or a sports team
☐ eat too much fat and sugar
☐ spend less time at the computer
[a] drink some chamomile tea
☐ study only the night before

a You should drink some chamomile tea.
b _____
c _____
d _____
e _____

one hundred ninety-five **195**

5 Use the verbs in the box and *should* or *shouldn't* to write internet safety tips.

> block   choose   download
> give out   log out   respond

a You _____ to offensive messages, even if they're from people you know.

b You _____ attachments from someone you don't know.

c You _____ suspicious people from your social media accounts.

d You _____ your password to anyone except your parents.

e You _____ from your accounts every time you finish checking them.

f You _____ a long password to protect your accounts and devices.

6 Complete the text with *should* or *shouldn't* and the correct form of the verbs in parentheses.

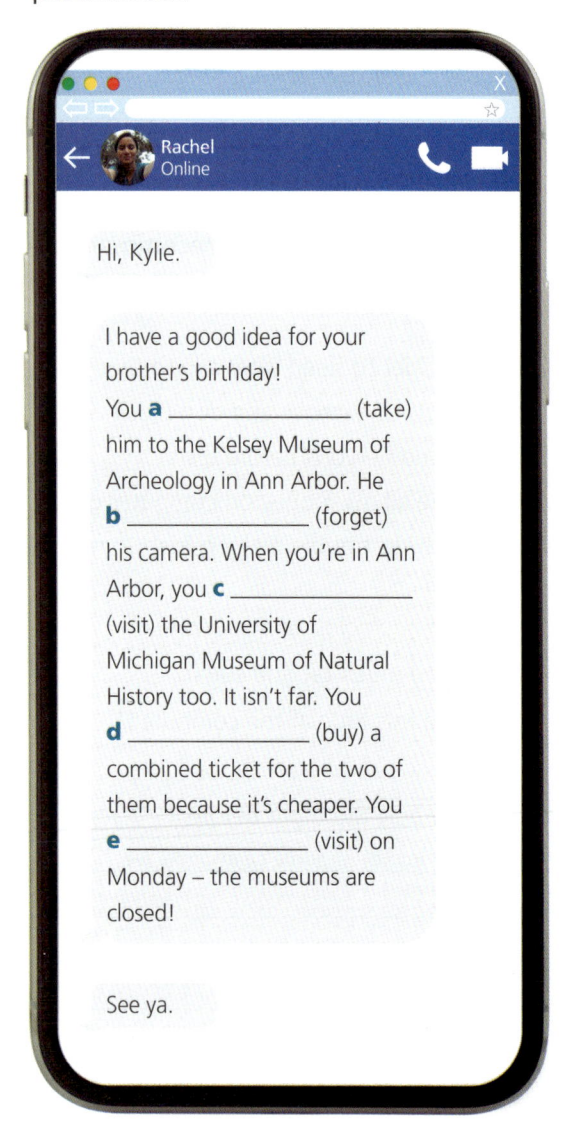

Rachel
Online

Hi, Kylie.

I have a good idea for your brother's birthday! You **a** _____ (take) him to the Kelsey Museum of Archeology in Ann Arbor. He **b** _____ (forget) his camera. When you're in Ann Arbor, you **c** _____ (visit) the University of Michigan Museum of Natural History too. It isn't far. You **d** _____ (buy) a combined ticket for the two of them because it's cheaper. You **e** _____ (visit) on Monday – the museums are closed!

See ya.

7 Write some recommendations on how to deal with guide dogs.

a You _____ make way for a guide dog and its owner.

b You _____ touch or pet the guide dog while it is on duty.

c You _____ respect the directions given by its owner at all times.

d You _____ the guide dog without its owner's authorization.

e You _____ the dog while it has its harness on.

f You _____ a guide dog organization.

8 Look at Jamila's notes and write sentences with *should* or *shouldn't*.

> eat pasta (✔)
> drink water (✔)
> go to school by car (✘)
> run every morning (✔)
> wear good sneakers (✔)
> run near cars (✘)

She should eat pasta.

a _____
b _____
c _____
d _____
e _____

UNIT 4

VOCABULARY 2

Health Problems

1 Look at the pictures and complete the words.

   a She has a c<u>old</u>_____.
   b He has a c_____.
   c He has a t_____.
   d She feels s_____.
   e He has a c_____.

2 Match a word in box A with a word in box B and write the health problems. Do you write them as one or two words?

   | A | ~~broken~~ ear head |
   | | insect sore stomach |

   | B | ache (×3) ~~arm~~ bite throat |

   broken arm
   a _____
   b _____
   c _____
   d _____
   e _____

3 Look at the pictures and complete the sentences with the words in the box. Then match the sentences a-f with the responses 1-6.

   | broken arm | cut | headache |
   | insect bite | sore throat | stomachache |

   a I have an _____ on my arm.

   b I have a _____ on my finger.

   c This _____ is terrible.

   d My _____ is getting worse.

   e I think I have a _____!

   f I have a _____ and I feel sick.

   1 Do you want some cough drops?
   2 Come on, let's go to the hospital.
   3 I think I have some special cream somewhere.
   4 Put on a bandage; there are some in the bathroom.
   5 Do you need an aspirin?
   6 Drink some water, then lie down.

one hundred ninety-seven **197**

GRAMMAR 2

should (Questions and Short Answers)

1 Order the words to make questions.

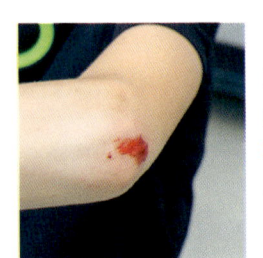

I / bandage / a / cut / Should / put / on / this ?
Should I put a bandage on this cut?
_____

a umbrella / take / Should / I / an ?
_____
_____
_____

b some / give / they / Should / pizza / dog / to / the ?
_____
_____
_____

c map / the / consult / they / Should ?
_____
_____
_____

d surprise / her / at / the / Should / we / party ?
_____
_____
_____

e mom / Should / for / I / money / ask / some ?
_____
_____
_____

2 Write short answers for the questions in activity 1, based on the pictures.

Yes, you should._____.

a _____
b _____
c _____
d _____
e _____

3 Complete the dialogue with *should* and the verbs in parentheses.

Ollie I have a test tomorrow and I can't remember anything. What **a** _____ (I / do)?

Teacher Well, first, **b** _____ (you / relax). **c** _____ (you / not get) stressed – it's bad for your memory. And **d** _____ (you / drink) water because water is good for your brain.

Ollie **e** _____ (I / study) late at night?

Teacher No, **f** _____ (you / not)! **g** _____ (you / sleep). But the most important thing is **h** _____ (you / not study) the night before the test. Your brain needs to rest!

198 one hundred ninety-eight

UNIT 4

GRAMMAR CHECK

1 Read the dialogue and circle the correct answers.

Liam My mom thinks I **a** ____ be an actor when I'm older. I love theater, but the problem is I get nervous when I perform.

Archie You should **b** ____ some classes, then.

Liam I'm busy with my math and science classes at the moment. I think I **c** ____ focus on these subjects first.

Archie If you don't have time to learn how to perform, **d** ____ study it. You **e** ____ think of a different profession! How about being an athlete? You're great at tennis.

Liam No, I want to be an actor. It isn't going to be easy, but I can do it. When I'm older, I'm going to look for theater classes.

Archie You **f** ____ at school. Mr. Simms knows about courses and professions.

Liam You **g** ____ worry so much, Archie. We're 14! Relax! Come on. Let's go and play tennis.

	1	2	3
a	shouldn't	(should)	should I
b	to take	take	taking
c	should	should to	shouldn't
d	should you	you aren't	you shouldn't
e	're going	should	shouldn't
f	ask	shouldn't ask	should ask
g	're going to	should	shouldn't

2 Listen and check your answers.

LISTENING

1 Listen to three telephone conversations. Circle the service each caller needs.

Caller 1: police   fire brigade   ambulance
Caller 2: police   fire brigade   ambulance
Caller 3: police   fire brigade   ambulance

2 Listen again and complete the chart with information about each caller.

	Caller 1
What is the problem?	
Where is the caller?	
What should the caller do?	

	Caller 2
What is the problem?	
Where is the caller?	
What should the caller do?	

	Caller 3
What is the problem?	
Where is the caller?	
What should the caller do?	

EXTENSION

Circle the correct options to complete the text.

Médecins Sans Frontières (Doctors Without Borders, in English) is an international non-governmental organization (NGO) that supports war-ravaged countries with medical care. Founded in 1971 by a group of French doctors and journalists, MSF **a has helped / have helped** several nations by providing them with medicine, donations, and the work of medical professionals.

Like many NGOs, MSF also needs to be supported in order to bring some comfort to people in need. What **b should you / you should** do to help the organization? First of all, you **c should to read / should read** as much information as possible on the MSF website, <https://www.doctorswithoutborders.org/>. You'll find detailed instructions about the various ways to contribute.

Money donation: the **d easiest / easier** way to support MSF is by donating money, since you can do it from anywhere in the world. One of the most important rules is that you **e shouldn't to / shouldn't** donate in any currency other than the United States dollars.

Royalty donation: an author, an actor, or a musician can help by donating the royalties from their work. They **f should / shouldn't** contact the Fundraising Events team by telephone or email to get started.

If you **g can't / should** donate anything but still think you **h should / shouldn't** help, you can publicize their work by sharing this information on your social media. Let's make a difference in people's lives.

UNIT 4

VOCABULARY PLUS

Places of Work

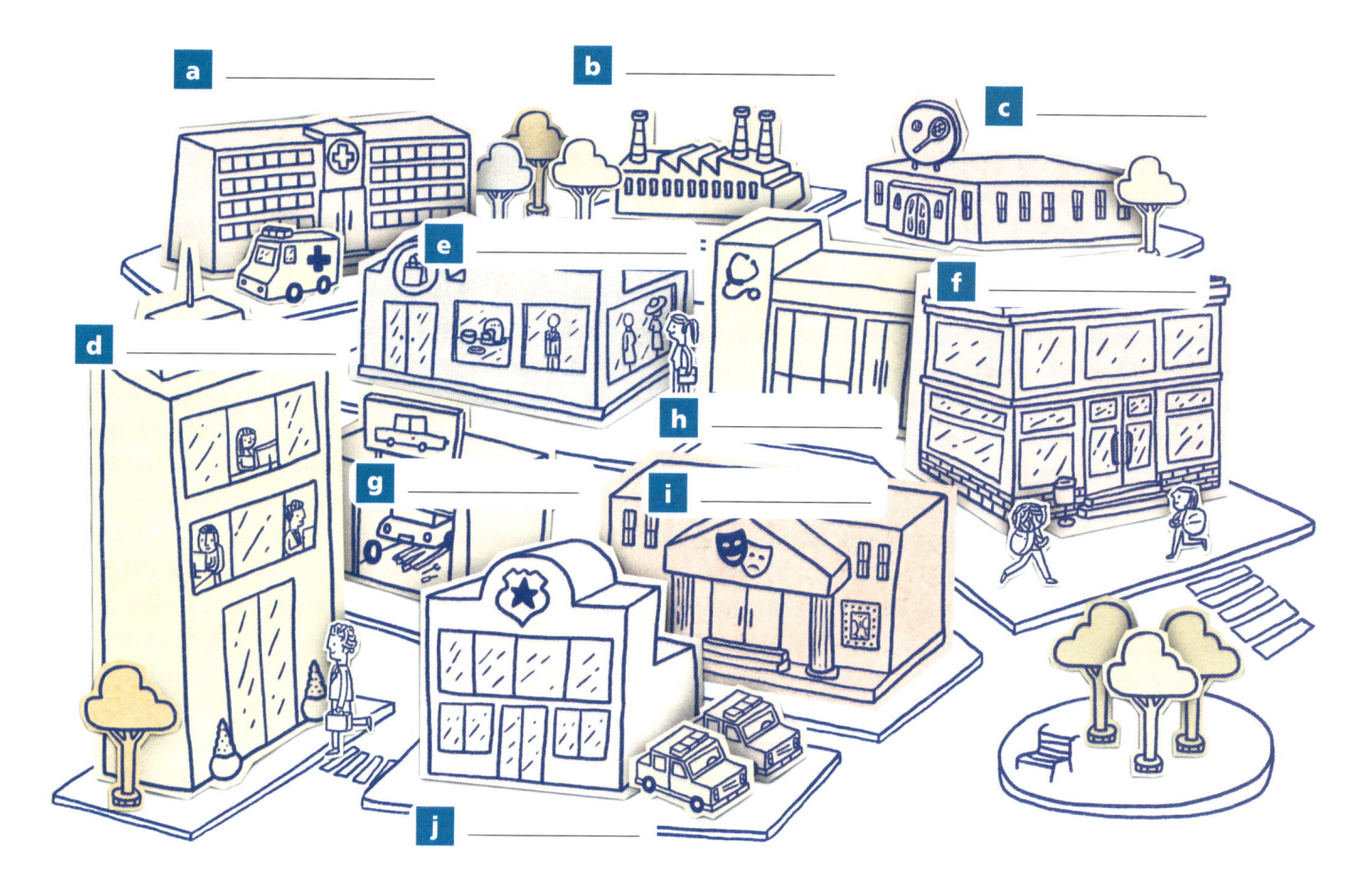

a _____ b _____ c _____
d _____ e _____ f _____
g _____ h _____ i _____
j _____

1 Look up the meaning of these words. Then listen and repeat.

department store	hospital
doctor's office	office
factory	police station
garage	sports club
high school	theater

2 Label the picture with the words in activity 1.

3 Match the jobs a-e with the places of work 1-5.

a actor
b police officer
c surgeon
d teacher
e mechanic

1 high school
2 garage
3 theater
4 hospital
5 police station

4 Underline the correct options.

When I'm older, I'm going to be a history teacher in a **high school** / **police station**.

a When my dog was ill, I took him to the vet's **garage** / **office**.

b My uncle sells computers in a very large **department store** / **theater**.

c My sister loves cars. She goes to our cousin's **garage** / **surgery** on Saturdays.

d The **office** / **factory** in our town makes paper.

5 Answer the questions for you. Write full sentences.

a Is there a theater in your town? Where is it?
_____

b How many high schools are there in your town?
_____

c How often do you go to the sports club? What do you do there?
_____

two hundred and one **201**

WORDLIST

PHONETIC CHART

25))) **VOWELS AND DIPHTHONGS**
/ɪ/ p**i**g /e/ br**ea**d /u/ l**o**se /aɪ/ **I**
/i/ sh**e** /ɜr/ c**ur**ly /ə/ act**o**r /ɔɪ/ t**oy**
/æ/ c**a**t /ɔ/ b**a**ll /ʌ/ s**u**nny /aʊ/ m**ou**ntain
/ɑ/ **ar**m /ʊ/ g**oo**d /eɪ/ US**A** /oʊ/ b**oa**t

26))) **CONSONANTS**
/p/ **p**otato /tʃ/ **ch**air /s/ **S**pain /n/ **n**ewsstand
/b/ **b**lue /dʒ/ fri**dge** /z/ ea**s**y /ŋ/ spri**ng**
/t/ **t**axi /f/ **f**inish /ʃ/ **sh**ower /l/ **l**ake
/d/ **d**rama /v/ **v**erb /ʒ/ televi**s**ion /r/ **r**ead
/k/ **c**arrot /θ/ ba**th**room /h/ **h**i /j/ **y**esterday
/g/ **g**randpa /ð/ **th**ere /m/ **m**outh /w/ **w**ater

27))) **A**
acoustic guitar (n) /əˈkustɪk ɡɪˈtar/
across (prep) /əˈkrɔs/
action-adventure (n) /ˈækʃ(ə)n ədˈventʃər/
actor (n) /ˈæktər/
advertise (v) /ˈædvərˌtaɪz/
advertisement (n) /ædˈvɜrtɪsmənt/
along (prep) /əˈlɔŋ/
already (adv) /ɔlˈredi/
also (adv) /ˈɔlsoʊ/
aluminum (n) /əˈlumɪnəm/
anniversary (n) /ˌænɪˈvɜrs(ə)ri/
annoy (v) /əˈnɔɪ/
annoyed (adj) /əˈnɔɪd/
annoying (adj) /əˈnɔɪɪŋ/
answer (v) /ˈænsər/
apartheid (n) /əˈpartˌhaɪt/
appear (v) /əˈpɪr/
architect (n) /ˈarkɪˌtekt/
argue (v) /ˈarˌgju/
argument (n) /ˈargjəmənt/
around (prep) /əˈraʊnd/
artist (n) /ˈartɪst/
ask (v) /æsk/
ate (v) /eɪt/
athlete (n) /ˈæθˌlit/
ATM (automated teller machine) (n) /ˌeɪ ti ˈem/
autograph (n) /ˈɔtəˌgræf/
autumn (n) /ˈɔtəm/
avalanche (n) /ˈævəˌlæntʃ/
award (n) /əˈwɔrd/
away from (prep) /əˈweɪ frəm/

28))) **B**
bag (n) /bæg/
be (v) /bi/
be born (v) /bi bɔrn/
be going to /bi ˈgoʊɪŋ tu/
because (conj) /bɪˈkɔz/
began (v) /bɪˈgæn/
begin (v) /bɪˈgɪn/
bill (n) /bɪl/
biomedicine (n) /ˈbaɪoʊˌmedɪsɪn/
birth (n) /bɜrθ/
birthday celebration (n) /ˈbɜrθˌdeɪ ˌseləˈbreɪʃ(ə)n/
blind (adj) /blaɪnd/
blizzard (n) /ˈblɪzərd/
boots (n) /buts/
bore (v) /bɔr/
bored (adj) /bɔrd/
boring (adj) /ˈbɔrɪŋ/
bottle (n) /ˈbɑt(ə)l/
box (n) /bɑks/
box office (n) /bɑks ˈɔfɪs/
break (v) /breɪk/
bric-a-brac sale (n) /ˈbrɪkəˌbræk seɪl/
broken arm /ˈbroʊkən arm/
bulletproof vest (n) /ˈbʊlɪtˌpruf vest/
buy a house /baɪ ə haʊs/

29))) **C**
call (v) /kɔl/
can (n) /kæn/
cardboard (n) /ˈkardˌbɔrd/
carton (n) /ˈkart(ə)n/
cell phone (n) /sel foʊn/
chat (v) /tʃæt/
check (n) /tʃek/
chimpanzee (n) /ˌtʃɪmpænˈzi/
clean-tech (n) /klin tek/
cliff (n) /klɪf/
cloudy (adj) /ˈklaʊdi/
coast (n) /koʊst/
coat (n) /koʊt/
coin (n) /kɔɪn/
coin purse (n) /kɔɪn pɜrs/

234 two hundred thirty-four

WORDLIST

cold (n) /koʊld/
come (v) /kʌm/
compete (v) /kəmˈpit/
competition (n) /ˌkɑmpəˈtɪʃ(ə)n/
computer (n) /kəmˈpjutər/
connect (v) /kəˈnekt/
connection (n) /kəˈnekʃ(ə)n/
construction worker (n) /kənˈstrʌkʃ(ə)n ˈwɜrkər/
contaminated water (n) /kənˈtæmɪˌneɪtəd ˈwɔtər/
cotton (n) /ˈkɑt(ə)n/
cough (n) /kɑf/
cow (n) /kaʊ/
crash (v) /kræʃ/
crocodile (n) /ˈkrɑkəˌdaɪl/
cut (v) /kʌt/
cycle (v) /ˈsaɪk(ə)l/
cyclone (n) /ˈsaɪˌkloʊn/

30))) **D**

death (n) /deθ/
decorate (v) /ˈdekəˌreɪt/
decoration (n) /ˌdekəˈreɪʃ(ə)n/
department store (n) /dɪˈpɑrtmənt stɔr/
develop (v) /dɪˈveləp/
development (n) /dɪˈveləpmənt/
die (v) /daɪ/
digital media (n) /ˈdɪdʒɪt(ə)l ˈmidiə/
director (n) /dɪˈrektər/
disease (n) /dɪˈziz/
disposable glove (n) /dɪˈspoʊzəb(ə)l glʌv/
divorce (n) /dɪˈvɔrs/
do a sponsored swim /du ə ˈspɑnsərd swɪm/
do charity work /du ˈtʃerəti wɜrk/
do exercise /du ˈeksərˌsaɪz/
do homework /du ˈhoʊmˌwɜrk/
do nothing /du ˈnʌθɪŋ/
do someone a favor /du ˈsʌmwʌn ə ˈfeɪvər/
do your best /du jʊr best/
doctor (n) /ˈdɑktər/
dolphin (n) /ˈdɑlfɪn/
dot-com company (n) /ˌdɑtˈkɑm ˈkʌmpəni/
down (prep) /daʊn/
dress (n) /dres/
drive (v) /draɪv/
drown (v) /draʊn/
drums (n) /drʌmz/
dry (adj) /draɪ/

31))) **E**

earache (n) /ˈɪrˌeɪk/
earmuffs (n) /ˈɪrˌmʌfs/
earring (n) /ˈɪrɪŋ/
educate (v) /ˈedʒəˌkeɪt/
education (n) /ˌedʒəˈkeɪʃ(ə)n/
electric bass (n) /ɪˈlektrɪk beɪs/
electric guitar (n) /ɪˈlektrɪk ɡɪˈtɑr/
elephant (n) /ˈeləfənt/
engagement (n) /ɪnˈɡeɪdʒmənt/

engineer (n) /ˌendʒɪˈnɪr/
enjoy (v) /ɪnˈdʒɔɪ/
enjoyment (n) /ɪnˈdʒɔɪmənt/
equip (v) /ɪˈkwɪp/
escape (v) /ɪˈskeɪp/
ever (adv) /ˈevər/
excite (v) /ɪkˈsaɪt/
excited (adj) /ɪkˈsaɪtəd/
excitement (n) /ɪkˈsaɪtmənt/
exciting (adj) /ɪkˈsaɪtɪŋ/

32))) **F**

face mask (n) /feɪs mæsk/
factory (n) /ˈfækt(ə)ri/
feel (v) /fil/
fell (v) /fel/
film a scene /fɪlm ə sin/
financial service (n) /fɪˈnænʃ(ə)l ˈsɜrvɪs/
flew (v) /flu/
flute (n) /flut/
for (prep / conj) /fɔr/
found (v) /faʊnd/
friendship (n) /ˈfren(d)ʃɪp/
frighten (v) /ˈfraɪt(ə)n/
frightened (adj) /ˈfraɪt(ə)nd/
frightening (adj) /ˈfraɪt(ə)nɪŋ/
fundraising (n) /ˈfʌndˌreɪzɪŋ/

33))) **G**

games (n) /ɡeɪmz/
garage (n) /ɡəˈrɑʒ/
garage sale (n) /ɡəˈrɑʒ seɪl/
get (v) /ɡet/
get a job /ɡet ə dʒɑb/
get married /ɡet ˈmerid/
give (v) /ɡɪv/
glass (n) /ɡlæs/
glove (n) /ɡlʌv/
go (v) /ɡoʊ/
go to /ɡoʊ tu /
go to college /ɡoʊ tu ˈkɑlɪdʒ/
Good Deeds Day (n) /ɡʊd dids deɪ/
Goodwill Ambassador (n) /ɡʊdˈwɪl æmˈbæsədər/
got (v) /ɡɑt/
got stuck /ɡɑt stʌk/
grow (v) /ɡroʊ/

34))) **H**

hailstorm (n) /ˈheɪlˌstɔrm/
happen (v) /ˈhæpən/
have children /hæv ˈtʃɪldrən/
headache (n) /ˈhedˌeɪk/
hear (v) /hɪr/
heat wave (n) /hit weɪv/
helmet (n) /ˈhelmət/
hide (v) /haɪd/
high drama (n) /haɪ ˈdrɑmə/
high school (n) /haɪ skul/

high visibility jacket (n) /ˌhaɪ vɪzəˈbɪləti ˈdʒækət/
hold (v) /hoʊld/
Hollywood blockbuster (n) /ˈhɑliˌwʊd ˈblɑkˌbʌstər/
hospital (n) /ˈhɑspɪt(ə)l/
hot (adj) /hɑt/
how long /haʊ lɔŋ/

35))) I
inform (v) /ɪnˈfɔrm/
information (n) /ˌɪnfərˈmeɪʃ(ə)n/
insect bite (n) /ˈɪnˌsekt baɪt/
inspector (n) /ɪnˈspektər/
interest (n) /ˈɪntrəst/
interested (adj) /ˈɪntrəstɪd/
interesting (adj) /ˈɪntrəstɪŋ/
internet browser (n) /ˈɪntərˌnet ˈbraʊzər/
into (prep) /ˈɪntu/
introduce (v) /ˌɪntrəˈdus/
invite (v) /ɪnˈvaɪt/

36))) J
jacket (n) /ˈdʒækət/
Jamaica (n) /dʒəˈmeɪkə/
jar (n) /dʒɑr/
jeans (n) /dʒinz/
journalist (n) /ˈdʒɜrn(ə)lɪst/
just (adv) /dʒʌst/

37))) L
lawyer (n) /ˈlɔjər/
learn to drive /lɜrn tu draɪv/
leave home /liv hoʊm/
leave school /liv skul/
leopard (n) /ˈlepərd/
lie (v) /laɪ/
lion (n) /ˈlaɪən/
listen (v) /ˈlɪs(ə)n/
live (v) /lɪv/
look (v) /lʊk/
lost (v) /lɔst/
love (v) /lʌv/

38))) M
make (v) /meɪk/
make a decision /meɪk ə dɪˈsɪʒ(ə)n/
make a mistake /meɪk ə mɪˈsteɪk/
make friends /meɪk frendz/
make money /meɪk ˈmʌni/
make someone happy /meɪk ˈsʌmwʌn ˈhæpi/
make someone laugh /meɪk ˈsʌmwʌn læf/
manage (v) /ˈmænɪdʒ/
Maori (n) /ˈmaʊri/
market opportunity (n) /ˈmɑrkət ˌɑpərˈtunəti/
meanwhile (adv) /ˈminˌwaɪl/
mechanic (n) /məˈkænɪk/
medical field (n) /ˈmedɪk(ə)l fild/
metal (n) /ˈmet(ə)l/
mild (adj) /maɪld/

monkey (n) /ˈmʌŋki/
mountain range (n) /ˈmaʊnt(ə)n reɪndʒ/
movie premiere (n) /ˈmuvi prɪˈmɪr/
movie star (n) /ˈmuvi stɑr/
moviemaker (n) /ˈmuviˌmeɪkər/
moviemaking (n) /ˈmuviˌmeɪkɪŋ/
multiplex movie theater (n) /ˈmʌltɪˌpleks ˈmuvi ˈθiətər/
must (v) /mʌst/

39))) N
notice (v) /ˈnoʊtɪs/
nurse (n) /nɜrs/

40))) O
ocean (n) /ˈoʊʃ(ə)n/
office (n) /ˈɔfɪs/
online (adj) /ˈɑnˌlaɪn/
open (v) /ˈoʊpən/
orangutan (n) /ɔˈræŋəˌtæn/
out of (prep) /aʊt əv/
over (prep) /ˈoʊvər/
overall (n) /ˈoʊvərˌɔl/

41))) P
panda (n) /ˈpændə/
paper (n) /ˈpeɪpər/
pass (v) /pæs/
pay by credit card /peɪ baɪ ˈkredɪt kɑrd/
pay in cash /peɪ ɪn kæʃ/
percussion (n) /pərˈkʌʃ(ə)n/
phone (n) /foʊn/
piano (n) /piˈænoʊ/
PIN (n) /pɪn/
plot (n) /plɑt/
plug (v) /plʌg/
polar bear (n) /ˈpoʊlər ber/
police officer (n) /pəˈlis ˈɔfɪsər/
police station (n) /pəˈlis ˈsteɪʃ(ə)n/
politician (n) /ˌpɑləˈtɪʃ(ə)n/
pond (n) /pɑnd/
poor sanitation (n) /pʊr ˌsænɪˈteɪʃ(ə)n/
popcorn (n) /ˈpɑpˌkɔrn/
possess (v) /pəˈzes/
possession (n) /pəˈzeʃ(ə)n/
post a comment /poʊst ə ˈkɑˌment/
predict (v) /prɪˈdɪkt/
prediction (n) /prɪˈdɪkʃ(ə)n/
prepare (v) /prɪˈper/
producer (n) /prəˈdusər/
put (v) /pʊt/

42))) Q
queue (n) /kju/

43))) R
rain boot (n) /reɪn but/
rainy (adj) /ˈreɪni/
read an e-book /rid æn i-bʊk/

WORDLIST

researcher (n) /rɪˈsɜrtʃər/
recognize (v) /ˈrekəɡˌnaɪz/
recycle (v) /riˈsaɪk(ə)l/
reduce (v) /rɪˈdus/
refer (v) /rɪˈfɜr/
release a movie /rɪˈlis ə ˈmuvi/
retirement (n) /rɪˈtaɪrmənt/
reuse (v) /ˌriˈjuz/
rhinoceros (n) /raɪˈnɑsərəs/
Royal Bengal Tiger (n) /ˈrɔɪəl ˈbeŋɡəl ˈtaɪɡər/

44 🔊 S

safety glasses (n) /ˈseɪfti ˈɡlæsəz/
sandal (n) /ˈsænd(ə)l/
saxophone (n) /ˈsæksəˌfoʊn/
scan a picture /skæn ə ˈpɪktʃər/
scarf (n) /skɑrf/
science fiction (n) /ˈsaɪəns ˈfɪkʃ(ə)n/
scientist (n) /ˈsaɪəntɪst/
script (n) /skrɪpt/
seat (n) /sit/
see (v) /si/
shark attack (n) /ʃɑrk əˈtæk/
shirt (n) /ʃɜrt/
shorts (n) /ʃɔrts/
should (v) /ʃʊd/
show (v) /ʃoʊ/
sick (adj) /sɪk/
since (adv / conj / prep) /sɪns/
Singapore (n) /ˈsɪŋəˌpɔr/
skirt (n) /skɜrt/
slipper (n) /ˈslɪpər/
smart TV (n) /smɑrt ˌtiˈvi/
smile (v) /smaɪl/
snake (n) /sneɪk/
sneakers (n) /ˈsnikərz/
snowy (adj) /ˈsnoʊi/
so (adv / conj) /soʊ/
soft drink (n) /sɔft drɪŋk/
soon (adv) /sun/
sore throat (n) /sɔr θroʊt/
soundtrack (n) /ˈsaʊn(d)ˌtræk/
South Africa (n) /saʊθ ˈæfrɪkə/
special effects (n) /ˈspeʃ(ə)l ɪˈfekts/
sports club (n) /spɔrts klʌb/
spring (n) /sprɪŋ/
star in a movie /stɑr ɪn ə ˈmuvi/
start school /stɑrt skul/
stay (v) /steɪ/
stomachache (n) /ˈstʌmək eɪk/
stop (v) /stɑp/
store (n) /stɔr/
stormy (adj) /ˈstɔrmi/
stream (n) /strim/
study (v) /ˈstʌdi/
study abroad (n) /ˈstʌdi əˈbrɔd/
stunt (n) /stʌnt/

suddenly (adv) /ˈsʌd(ə)nli/
suggest (v) /səɡˈdʒest/
suggestion (n) /səɡˈdʒestʃ(ə)n/
summer (n) /ˈsʌmər/
sun hat (n) /sʌn hæt/
sunny (adj) /ˈsʌni/
surf (v) /sɜrf/
surgeon (n) /ˈsɜrdʒən/
surprise (v) /sərˈpraɪz/
surprised (adj) /sərˈpraɪzd/
surprising (adj) /sərˈpraɪzɪŋ/
survive (v) /sərˈvaɪv/
swam (v) /swæm/
sweater (n) /ˈswetər/
swim (v) /swɪm/

45 🔊 T

take (v) /teɪk/
talk (v) /tɔk/
teacher (n) /ˈtitʃər/
technician (n) /tekˈnɪʃ(ə)n/
technology sector (n) /tekˈnɑlədʒi ˈsektər/
tell (v) /tel/
temperature (n) /ˈtemp(ə)rəˌtʃʊr/
theater (n) /ˈθiətər/
then (adj / adv) /ðen/
think (v) /θɪŋk/
thunderstorm (n) /ˈθʌndərˌstɔrm/
ticket (n) /ˈtɪkɪt/
tie (n) /taɪ/
tiger (n) /ˈtaɪɡər/
tip (n) /tɪp/
tire (v) /ˈtaɪr/
tired (adj) /ˈtaɪrd/
tiring (adj) /ˈtaɪrɪŋ/
tomorrow (adv) /təˈmɔroʊ/
too (adv) /tu/
took (v) /tʊk/
towards (prep) /tɔrdz/
train to be a /treɪn tu bi ə/
Trinidad and Tobago (n) /ˈtrɪnɪˌdæd ænd təˈbeɪɡoʊ/
trumpet (n) /ˈtrʌmpət/
try (v) /traɪ/
T-shirt (n) /ti-ʃɜrt/
turtle (n) /ˈtɜrt(ə)l/

46 🔊 U

umbrella (n) /ʌmˈbrelə/
under (prep) /ˈʌndər/
up (prep) /ʌp/
upload (v) /ˈʌpˌloʊd/
URL (n) /ˌju ɑr ˈel/
use (v) /juz/

47 🔊 V

valley (n) /ˈvæli/
vet (n) /vet/

video game (n) /ˈvɪdioʊ geɪm/
violin (n) /ˌvaɪəˈlɪn/
visor (n) /ˈvaɪzər/

48))) W

wait (v) /weɪt/
want (v) /wɑnt/
warm (adj) /wɔrm/
was (v) /wɑz/
wash cars /wɑʃ kɑrz/
water molecule (n) /ˈwɔtər ˈmɑləˌkjul/
water service (n) /ˈwɔtər ˈsɜrvɪs/
waterproof (n) /ˈwɔtərˌpruf/
waterproof jacket (n) /ˈwɔtərˌpruf ˈdʒækət/
wave (n) /weɪv/
wear (v) /wer/
web page (n) /ˈweb peɪdʒ/
website (n) /ˈwebˌsaɪt/
wedding (n) /ˈwedɪŋ/
were (v) /wɜr/
wet (adj) /wet/
while (conj) /waɪl/
wildfire (n) /ˈwaɪldˌfaɪr/
will (v) /wɪl/
win an award /wɪn æn əˈwɔrd/
windy (adj) /ˈwɪndi/
winter (n) /ˈwɪntər/
wool (n) /wʊl/
work (v) /wɜrk/
work with children /wɜrk wɪð ˈtʃɪldrən/
World Water Day (n) /wɜrld ˈwɔtər deɪ/
World Wide Web (n) /wɜrld waɪd web/
worried (adj) /ˈwʌrid/
worry (v) /ˈwʌri/
worrying (adj) /ˈwʌriɪŋ/
write (v) /raɪt/

49))) Y

yard sale (n) /jɑrd seɪl/
yet (adv) /jet/

2022 © Macmillan Education Brasil

Based on *InstaEnglish* and *Motivate*
© Macmillan Education Brasil 2019 and Macmillan Education Limited 2013
Written by Emma Heyderman, Fiona Mauchline, Patrick Howarth, Patricia Reilly and Olivia Johnston
Grammar, *Speaking*, and *Culture* pages adapted by Gisele Marçon Bastos Périgo and Thelma de Carvalho Guimarães
Vocabulary, *Reading*, and *Writing* pages adapted by Thelma de Carvalho Guimarães
Digital Literacy and *Global Citizenship* pages created by Thelma de Carvalho Guimarães

Director of Languages Brazil: Patricia Souza De Luccia
Publishing Manager and Field Researcher: Patricia Muradas
Content Creation Coordinator: Cristina do Vale
Art Coordinator: Jean Aranha
Lead Editors: Gabriel França, Roberta Somera
Content Editors: Ana Beatriz da Costa Moreira, Gabriel França, Roberta Somera, Tatiana Martins Santana
Digital Editors: Deborah Stafussi, Elaine Lins
Editorial Assistant: Carolina Araújo de Melo, Daniela Alves
Editorial Intern: Pedro Improta
Art Assistant: Jacqueline Alves
Art Intern: Victor Augusto Amorim
Editorial Apprentice: Beatriz Jacinto
Graphic Production: Alexandra L. S. de Carvalho, Thais Mendes P. Galvão
Proofreaders: Ana Lúcia Mendes Reis, Cátia de Almeida, Edward Willson, Rhiannon Ball
Design Concept: Martha Tadaieski
Page Makeup: Figurattiva Editorial
Photo Research: Marcia Sato
Illustrations: Bruna Assis
Image Processing: Jacqueline Alves, Jean Aranha, Victor Augusto Amorim
Extra Interactive Activities Content Development: Daniela Alves
Cover Concept: Jean Aranha
Cover photography: BartekSzewczyk/iStockphoto/Getty Images
Audio: Argila
Video: Desenredo

Reproduction prohibited. Penal Code Article 184 and Law number 9.610 of February 19, 1998.

We would like to dedicate this book to teachers all over Brazil. We would also like to thank our clients and teachers who have helped us make this book better with their many rich contributions and feedback straight from the classroom!

The authors, adaptor and publishers would like to thank the following for permission to reproduce the photographic material:
p. 8: PeopleImages/iStockphoto/Getty Images. p. 9 shapecharge/iStockphoto/Getty Images; PeopleImages/iStockphoto/Getty Images. p. 10: metamorworks/iStockphoto/Getty Images. p. 12: THEPALMER/iStockphoto/Getty Images; JM_Image_Factory/iStockphoto/Getty Images; Chaay_Tee/iStockphoto/Getty Images; fizkes/iStockphoto/Getty Images; Capuski/iStockphoto/Getty Images; XH4D/iStockphoto/Getty Images; Yulia Sutyagina/iStockphoto/Getty Images; DaniloAndjus/iStockphoto/Getty Images. p. 14: bakalusha/iStockphoto/Getty Images; Andranik Hakobyan/iStockphoto/Getty Images; monkeybusinessimages/iStockphoto/Getty Images. p. 15: hocus-focus/iStockphoto/Getty Images. p. 16: FG Trade/iStockphoto/Getty Images; Capuski/iStockphoto/Getty Images; alvarez/iStockphoto/Getty Images; PIKSEL/iStockphoto/Getty Images; South_agency/iStockphoto/Getty Images. p. 17: Nikada/iStockphoto/Getty Images; Kandl/iStockphoto/Getty Images. p. 18: andreswd/iStockphoto/Getty Images; kali9/iStockphoto/Getty Images; ogiana/iStockphoto/Getty Images; andresr/iStockphoto/Getty Images; LanaStock/iStockphoto/Getty Images; skynesher/iStockphoto/Getty Images; kali9/iStockphoto/Getty Images; jeffbergen/iStockphoto/Getty Images; mixetto/iStockphoto/Getty Images; Drazen Zigic/iStockphoto/Getty Images; MAGNIFIER/iStockphoto/Getty Images; PeopleImages/iStockphoto/Getty Images; shironosov/iStockphoto/Getty Images; Hispanolistic/iStockphoto/Getty Images; VectorMine/iStockphoto/Getty Images. p. 21: VectorMine/iStockphoto/Getty Images; solarisimages/iStockphoto/Getty Images. p. 23: Andrey Suslov/iStockphoto/Getty Images. p. 24: yktr/iStockphoto/Getty Images. p. 25: Chaay_Tee/iStockphoto/Getty Images.; JM_Image_Factory/iStockphoto/Getty Images; Jirsak/iStockphoto/Getty Images; gopixa/iStockphoto/Getty Images; Capuski/iStockphoto/Getty Images; XH4D/iStockphoto/Getty Images; fizkes/iStockphoto/Getty Images; THEPALMER/iStockphoto/Getty Images; kali9/iStockphoto/Getty Images; ogiana/iStockphoto/Getty Images; andresr/iStockphoto/Getty Images; LanaStock/iStockphoto/Getty Images; kali9/iStockphoto/Getty Images; jeffbergen/iStockphoto/Getty Images; Drazen Zigic/iStockphoto/Getty Images; MAGNIFIER/iStockphoto/Getty Images; Hispanolistic/iStockphoto/Getty Images; Mario Ruiz / ZUMA PRESS / Imageplus; Imago/ ZUMA PRESS / Imageplus; Adrian Boot / Retna / Photoshot / UPPA / ZUMA PRESS / Imageplus; Jaqueline Goes/Acervo pessoal; Daniel Karmann / DPA / ZUMA Press / Imageplus; Jon Gambrell / AP Photo / Imageplus. p. 26: vikarus/iStockphoto/Getty Images. p. 28: miskani/iStockphoto/Getty Images; lemga/iStockphoto/Getty Images; slowmotiongli/iStockphoto/Getty Images; stanley45/iStockphoto/Getty Images; sidneybernstein/iStockphoto/Getty Images. p. 29: filborg/iStockphoto/Getty Images; PeopleImages/iStockphoto/Getty Images; Gerald Corsi/iStockphoto/Getty Images; Mystockimages/iStockphoto/Getty Images; vnarong/iStockphoto/Getty Images; Maryna Rayimova/iStockphoto/Getty Images. p. 30: PCH-Vector/iStockphoto/Getty Images. p. 31: Whitepointer/iStockphoto/Getty Images. p. 32: monkeybusinessimages/iStockphoto/Getty Images. p. 33: master2/iStockphoto/Getty Images; JeremyRichards/iStockphoto/Getty Images; swissfoto/iStockphoto/Getty Images; ChandrashekarReddy/iStockphoto/Getty Images; Matrishva Vyas/iStockphoto/Getty Images. p. 35: sharply_done/iStockphoto/Getty Images. p. 40: RamonCarretero/iStockphoto/Getty Images. p. 41: fotografixx/iStockphoto/Getty Images; Kobus Louw/iStockphoto/Getty Images; ozgurcankaya/iStockphoto/Getty Images; PeopleImages/iStockphoto/Getty Images; SB Arts Media/iStockphoto/Getty Images; golubovy/iStockphoto/Getty Images; FG Trade/iStockphoto/Getty Images; Prostock-Studio/iStockphoto/Getty Images; gilaxia/iStockphoto/Getty Images; RuslanDashinsky/iStockphoto/Getty Images; altmodern/iStockphoto/Getty Images; Giselleflissak/iStockphoto/Getty Images Jetta Productions/iStockphoto/Getty Images; Bojan89/iStockphoto/Getty Images; Povozniuk/iStockphoto/Getty Images; FG Trade/iStockphoto/Getty Images. p. 42: FG Trade/iStockphoto/Getty Images; SHansche/iStockphoto/Getty Images; ajr_images/iStockphoto/Getty Images; FG Trade/iStockphoto/Getty Images; JPWALLET/iStockphoto/Getty Images; kickstand/iStockphoto/Getty Images; jukov/iStockphoto/Getty Images; BassittART/iStockphoto/Getty Images; martin-dm/iStockphoto/Getty Images; MariuszSzczygiel/iStockphoto/Getty Images. p. 43: undrey/iStockphoto/Getty Images; AndreyPopov/iStockphoto/Getty Images; SDI Productions/iStockphoto/Getty Images; gorodenkoff/iStockphoto/Getty Images SDI Productions/iStockphoto/Getty Images; chinaface/iStockphoto/Getty Images; AndreyPopov/iStockphoto/Getty Images; shironosov/iStockphoto/Getty Images; SB Arts Media/iStockphoto/Getty Images; BlackSalmon/iStockphoto/Getty Images. p. 46: lushik/iStockphoto/Getty Images; _human/iStockphoto/Getty Images; Avector/iStockphoto/Getty Images; fad1986/iStockphoto/Getty Images. p. 48: Youngoldman/iStockphoto/Getty Images. p. 50: wckiw/iStockphoto/Getty Images; skynesher/iStockphoto/Getty Images; Brothers91/iStockphoto/Getty Images; Roll6/iStockphoto/Getty Images; Halfpoint/iStockphoto/Getty Images; ArtMarie/iStockphoto/Getty Images. p. 51: martin-dm/iStockphoto/Getty Images; Pixilated Planet/iStockphoto/Getty Images; Robin Rayne / ZUMA Press / Imageplus. p.52: Ulzanna/iStockphoto/Getty Images; Pollyana Ventura/iStockphoto/Getty Images. p. 54: MesquitaFMS/iStockphoto/Getty Images; avdeev007/iStockphoto/Getty Images; yoh4nn/iStockphoto/Getty Images. p. 55: Carl Henry ©2004/iStockphoto/Getty Images; Jodi Jacobson/iStockphoto/Getty Images. p. 56: Ирина Руденко/iStockphoto/Getty Images; WeiseMaxHelloween/iStockphoto/Getty Images golero/iStockphoto/Getty Images; Imgorthand/iStockphoto/Getty Images. p. 57: Steve C. Mitchell / Invision / AP Photo / Imageplus; 400tmax/iStockphoto/Getty Images; monkeybusinessimages/iStockphoto/Getty Images; svetikd/iStockphoto/Getty Images. p. 59: falun/iStockphoto/Getty Images; Bob Hilscher/iStockphoto/Getty Images; Kirsty O'Connor/AP Photo/Image Plus; p. 61: tbgrant/iStockphoto/Getty Images; AnnaFrajtova/iStockphoto/Getty Images; SolStock/iStockphoto/Getty Images. p. 62: Evgeny Sergeev/iStockphoto/Getty Images. p. 63: rolleiflextlr/iStockphoto/Getty Images; prairie_eye/iStockphoto/Getty Images; Lidiya Buzuevskaya/iStockphoto/Getty Images; mawielobob/iStockphoto/Getty Images; popovaphoto/iStockphoto/Getty Images; Tarzhanova/iStockphoto/Getty Images; pearleye/iStockphoto/Getty Images; Elena Koroleva/iStockphoto/Getty Images; mawielobob/iStockphoto/Getty Images; FlamingPumpkin/iStockphoto/Getty Images; iprachenko/iStockphoto/Getty Images; NadiaCruzova/iStockphoto/Getty Images; sankai/iStockphoto/Getty Images; WeiseMaxHelloween/iStockphoto/Getty Images; Ирина Руденко/iStockphoto/Getty Images; golero/iStockphoto/Getty Images; Imgorthand/iStockphoto/Getty Images; bgfoto/iStockphoto/Getty Images; Imgorthand/iStockphoto/Getty Images; montreehanlue/iStockphoto/Getty Images; Marc Bruxelle/iStockphoto/Getty Images; lovemovement/iStockphoto/Getty Images; Willowpix/iStockphoto/Getty Images; MD_Art/iStockphoto/Getty Images; momnoi/iStockphoto/Getty Images; mdphoto16/iStockphoto/Getty Images; LuckyBusiness/iStockphoto/Getty Images; Angelo D'Amico/iStockphoto/Getty Images. p. 64: Capuski/iStockphoto/Getty Images. p. 66: Tenedos/iStockphoto/Getty Images; xavierarnau/iStockphoto/Getty Images; LightFieldStudios/iStockphoto/Getty Images; Ridofranz/iStockphoto/Getty Images; spb2015/iStockphoto/Getty Images; JuFagundes/iStockphoto/Getty Images. p. 67: ThitareeSarmkasat/iStockphoto/Getty Images; Sonia Moskowitz / ZUMA Press / Imageplus. p. 68: Cristian Borrego Sala/iStockphoto/Getty Images. p. 69: Volodymyr Rozumii/iStockphoto/Getty Images; Avalon_Studio/iStockphoto/Getty Images; SolStock/iStockphoto/Getty Images; PhilAugustavo/iStockphoto/Getty Images Cecilia Fabiano / LaPresse / ZUMA Press / Imageplus; Kyodo / AP Photo / Imageplus; Daniel de la Hoz/iStockphoto/Getty Images. p. 70: Courtney Hale/iStockphoto/Getty Images; Nadezhda Ivanova/iStockphoto/Getty Images; exxorian/iStockphoto/Getty Images; filo/iStockphoto/Getty Images. p. 71: Isabella/iStockphoto/Getty Images; pavalena/iStockphoto/Getty Images. p. 72: PeopleImages/iStockphoto/Getty Images. p. 73: PeopleImages/iStockphoto/Getty Images; VioletaStoimenova/iStockphoto/Getty Images; AntonioGuillem/iStockphoto/Getty Images; Antonio_Diaz/iStockphoto/Getty Images; dorioconnell/iStockphoto/Getty Images; Brothers91/iStockphoto/Getty Images. p. 75: monkeybusinessimages/iStockphoto/Getty Images; mediaphotos/iStockphoto/Getty Images. p.77: FatCamera/iStockphoto/Getty Images; AJ_Watt/iStockphoto/Getty Images; glebchik/iStockphoto/Getty Images; Hiraman/iStockphoto/Getty Images; Inside Creative House/iStockphoto/Getty Images; herraez/iStockphoto/Getty Images. p. 78: FG Trade/iStockphoto/Getty Images. p. 79: LightFieldStudios/iStockphoto/Getty Images; FatCamera/iStockphoto/Getty Images; Tenedos/iStockphoto/Getty Images; AJ_Watt/iStockphoto/Getty Images; glebchik/iStockphoto/Getty Images; Hiraman/iStockphoto/Getty Images; spb2015/iStockphoto/Getty Images; JuFagundes/iStockphoto/Getty Images; Ridofranz/iStockphoto/Getty Images; Inside Creative House/iStockphoto/Getty Images; xavierarnau/iStockphoto/Getty Images; herraez/iStockphoto/Getty Images. p. 80: LightFieldStudios/iStockphoto/Getty Images; Imgorthand/iStockphoto/Getty Images; dragana991/iStockphoto/Getty Images; Marc Bruxelle/iStockphoto/Getty Images. p. 81: Hiraman/iStockphoto/Getty Images; JuFagundes/iStockphoto/Getty Images; Willowpix/iStockphoto/Getty Images; momnoi/iStockphoto/Getty Images; Angelo D'Amico/iStockphoto/Getty Images. p. 83: Liubomyr Vorona/iStockphoto/Getty Images. p. 84: atakan/iStockphoto/Getty Images. p. 86: andresr/iStockphoto/Getty Images; Ridofranz/iStockphoto/Getty Images. p. 168: Serghei Starus/iStockphoto/Getty Images; -slav-/iStockphoto/Getty Images. p. 169: andrelteixeira/iStockphoto/Getty Images. p. 170: grinvalds/iStockphoto/Getty Images; Weedezign/iStockphoto/Getty Images; gorodenkoff/iStockphoto/Getty Images; p.Kijsanayothin/iStockphoto/Getty Images; Tippapatt/iStockphoto/Getty Images; hocus-focus/iStockphoto/Getty Images; praetorianphoto/iStockphoto/Getty Images. p. 171: APPhoto/Ben Margot,File. p. 173: Daniel Tadevosyan/iStockphoto/Getty Images; markp73/iStockphoto/Getty Images; JoyImage/iStockphoto/Getty Images; Brandon Wood/iStockphoto/Getty Images; Tevarak/iStockphoto/Getty Images; Zolnierek/iStockphoto/Getty Images; 9dreamstudio/iStockphoto/Getty Images; KTM_2016/iStockphoto/Getty Images. p. 175: jacoblund/iStockphoto/Getty Images; bowie15/iStockphoto/Getty Images. p. 176: FG Trade/iStockphoto/Getty Images; p. 179: OlafSpeier/iStockphoto/Getty Images. p. 181: elenaleonova/iStockphoto/Getty Images; MachineHeadz/iStockphoto/Getty Images; AnnaStills/iStockphoto/Getty Images; fizkes/iStockphoto/Getty Images; YinYang/iStockphoto/Getty Images; zamrznutitonovi/iStockphoto/Getty Images; AndreyPopov/iStockphoto/Getty Images; Bigandt_Photography/iStockphoto/Getty Images; AntonioGuillem/iStockphoto/Getty Images; danchooalex/iStockphoto/Getty Images. p. 183: Benjamas Suwanmanee/iStockphoto/Getty Images. p. 185: Lysogor/iStockphoto/Getty Images; Anneliese Gruenwald-Maerkl/iStockphoto/Getty Images; Ig0rZh/iStockphoto/Getty Images; Dimple Bhati/iStockphoto/Getty Images; dovate/iStockphoto/Getty Images; rommma/iStockphoto/Getty Images; Zenobillis/iStockphoto/Getty Images; traveler1116/iStockphoto/Getty Images; Maxiphoto/iStockphoto/Getty Images; Adrian Wojcik/iStockphoto/Getty Images. p. 186: Lilkin/iStockphoto/Getty Images; Liudmila Chernetska/iStockphoto/Getty Images; vav63/iStockphoto/Getty Images; Michael Burrell/iStockphoto/Getty Images; Tarzhanova/iStockphoto/Getty Images; Vitalily73/iStockphoto/Getty Images; MarisaLia/iStockphoto/Getty Images; nikkytok/iStockphoto/Getty Images; Green_Leaf/iStockphoto/Getty Images; clu/iStockphoto/Getty Images; Aliaksandr Litviniuk/iStockphoto/Getty Images; DmitriyTitov/iStockphoto/Getty Images; SomeMeans/iStockphoto/Getty Images. p. 187: monkeybusinessimages/iStockphoto/Getty Images. p.188: swissmediavision/iStockphoto/Getty Images. p. 189: DieterMeyrl/iStockphoto/Getty Images; sankai/iStockphoto/Getty Images; Imgorthand/iStockphoto/Getty Images; MarianVejcik/iStockphoto/Getty Images; mdesigner125/iStockphoto/Getty Images; Tomas Ragina/iStockphoto/Getty Images; jeffbergen/iStockphoto/Getty Images; Andranik Hakobyan/iStockphoto/Getty Images; Trifonov_Evgeniy/iStockphoto/Getty Images; Milan Krasula/iStockphoto/Getty Images; Lucas Ninno/iStockphoto/Getty Images; rustamank/iStockphoto/Getty Images; spectrelabs/iStockphoto/Getty Images; omersukrugoksu/iStockphoto/Getty Images; beyhanyazar/iStockphoto/Getty Images; Tuangtong/iStockphoto/Getty Images; omersukrugoksu/iStockphoto/Getty Images. p. 192: alessen/iStockphoto/Getty Images. p. 194: filrom/iStockphoto/Getty Images; PixelsEffect/iStockphoto/Getty Images; glebchik/iStockphoto/Getty Images; FG Trade/iStockphoto/Getty Images; shapecharge/iStockphoto/Getty Images. Oleksandra Polishchuk/iStockphoto/Getty Images. p. 195: digitalskillet/iStockphoto/Getty Images. p. 196: DisobeyArt; Deepak Sethi/iStockphoto/Getty Images; adogslifephoto/iStockphoto/Getty Images. p. 197: seb_ra/iStockphoto/Getty Images; Daisy-Daisy/iStockphoto/Getty Images; PaulBiryukov/iStockphoto/Getty Images; RealPeopleGroup/iStockphoto/Getty Images; Nebasin/iStockphoto/Getty Images; dorioconnell/iStockphoto/Getty Images; worac/iStockphoto/Getty Images; bymuratdeniz/iStockphoto/Getty Images; dragana991/iStockphoto/Getty Images; Jay Yuno/iStockphoto/Getty Images; LaylaBird/iStockphoto/Getty Images; Svetlana Larshina/iStockphoto/Getty Images. p. 198: JackF/iStockphoto/Getty Images;

Alena Ivochkina/iStockphoto/Getty Images; SimonSkafar/iStockphoto/Getty Images; LukaTDB/iStockphoto/Getty Images; AntonioGuillem/iStockphoto/Getty Images; FG Trade/iStockphoto/Getty Images; skynesher/iStockphoto/Getty Images. p. 199: SDI Productions/iStockphoto/Getty Images; M_a_y_a/iStockphoto/Getty Images. p. 200: AP Photo/Michel Euler.

```
Dados Internacionais de Catalogação na Publicação (CIP)
     (BENITEZ Catalogação Ass. Editorial, MS, Brasil)

I48        InstaEnglish 2nd edition level 2 student's
2.ed.        book and workbook : SPLIT A / Emma
             Heyderman...[et al.]. - 2.ed. -
             São Paulo : Macmillan Education do
             Brasil, 2023.
             136 p.; il.; 21 x 29,7 cm.

             Outros autores: Fiona Mauchline, Patrick
          Howarth, Patricia Reilly, Olivia Johnston.
             ISBN 978-65-5752-297-4

             1. Língua inglesa (Ensino fundamental).
          I. Mauchline, Fiona. II. Howarth, Patrick.
          III. Reilly, Patricia. IV. Johnston, Olivia.
05-2023/39                      CDD 372.652

            Índice para catálogo sistemático:
        1. Língua inglesa : Ensino fundamental   372.652
     Aline Graziele Benitez - Bibliotecária - CRB-1/3129
```

All rights reserved.

MACMILLAN EDUCATION BRASIL
Av. Brigadeiro Faria Lima, 1.309, 2º Andar
Jd. Paulistano – São Paulo – SP – 01452-002
www.macmillan.com.br
Customer Service: [55] (11) 4613-2278
0800 16 88 77

Printed in Brazil. First print. August, 2023.

Gráfica Eskenazi

NOTES

NOTES

NOTES

NOTES

NOTES

NOTES